AF715449

Introduction to Business Analytics

Student Edition

Kimberly Seefeld, EdD

Table of contents

Introduction to Business Analytics

Student Edition

By Kimberly Seefeld, EdD

Published under **DataJoyAI** imprint

Companion resources for this book are available at:

DataJoyAI

https://datajoyai.com

Edition: First Edition
ISBN: 978-1-969233-40-1

Chapter 1

Introduction to Business Analytics

1.1 Learning Outcomes

1-1. Define business analytics and identify the four main types

1-2. Recognize examples of business analytics in companies you know

1-3. Understand why businesses use data to make decisions

1-4. Identify how artificial intelligence helps businesses analyze data

1.2 Introduction

Every morning when you wake up and check your phone, you encounter business analytics without realizing it. The personalized news feed on your social media app, the music recommendations on Spotify, and even the route your GPS suggests to avoid

traffic are all products of companies using data to make decisions that affect your experience. Business analytics has become so integrated into our daily lives that we often take it for granted, yet understanding how it works can help you become a more informed consumer and a more valuable employee in almost any career you choose.

Business analytics is fundamentally about using information to make better business decisions. Rather than relying solely on intuition or guesswork, companies collect data about their customers, operations, and markets, then analyze this information to understand patterns and make smarter choices. This approach has transformed how businesses operate, from small local shops to multinational corporations.

Consider your favorite coffee shop as a simple example. The owner might notice that more customers order iced drinks on sunny days and hot beverages when it's raining. By tracking these patterns over time and combining them with weather forecasts, the owner can better predict demand and ensure they have the right products available when customers want them. This basic form of analytics helps the business serve customers better while reducing waste and increasing profits.

The impact of business analytics extends far beyond individual businesses. The global business analytics market has grown from $84.42 billion in 2024 to a projected $176.14 billion by 2031, representing a compound annual growth rate of 9.63%. This explosive growth reflects a fundamental shift in how organizations operate and compete. Companies that effectively use data to guide their decisions consistently outperform those that rely primarily on traditional methods.

Throughout this chapter, we will explore what business analytics means in practical terms, examine the four main types of analytics that companies use, look at real examples from businesses you interact with regularly, and understand how artificial intelligence is changing the way companies work with data. By the end of this module, you will be able to recognize analytics in action around you and understand why these skills have become essential in today's business environment.

1.3 Understanding Business Analytics

1.3.1 Defining Business Analytics

Business analytics is the systematic examination of data to help organizations make informed decisions. At its core, it involves three fundamental steps: collecting relevant information, organizing that information in meaningful ways, and analyzing it to discover patterns or insights that can guide business actions. This process transforms raw data into actionable knowledge that companies can use to improve their operations, better serve their customers, and increase their competitiveness.

The concept becomes clearer when we consider a concrete example. Imagine you manage a small restaurant and notice that your weekend dinner sales have been declining over the past few months. Without analytics, you might simply guess the cause or make changes based on assumptions. However, with a business analytics approach, you would systematically gather information about various factors that might influence your sales. You might examine your sales data by day of the week and time of day, review customer feedback and online reviews, analyze local events and competition, and consider external factors like weather patterns or economic conditions.

Once you have collected this information, you will organize it in a way that allows you to see patterns and relationships. You might create charts showing sales trends over time, compare your performance to local events or competitor activities, and categorize customer feedback by themes. Finally, you would analyze this organized information to identify the most likely causes of your sales decline and develop strategies to address them.

This systematic approach to problem-solving distinguishes business analytics from simple reporting or casual observation. While a basic sales report might tell you that revenue decreased by fifteen percent last month, business analytics would help you understand why this happened and what you can do about it. The goal is not just to describe what occurred, but to gain insights that enable better decision-making in the future.

1.3.2 The Data Revolution in Business

Every interaction between businesses and customers generates data that can be analyzed for insights. When you make a purchase online, visit a website, use a mobile app, call customer service, or even walk through a store, you create information that businesses can collect and analyze. The challenge for companies is not finding data, but rather determining which data is most valuable and how to extract meaningful insights from it.

Modern technology has dramatically increased both the volume of available data and the tools for analyzing it. Point-of-sale systems capture detailed information about every transaction, websites track user behavior in real-time, mobile apps monitor usage patterns, and social media platforms provide insights into customer preferences and opinions. This wealth of information provides unprecedented opportunities for businesses to understand their customers and optimize their operations.

However, having access to data is only the beginning. The real value comes from transforming this raw information into actionable insights. This requires not only technical tools and skills, but also business knowledge to ask the right questions and interpret results in meaningful ways. Companies that excel at this transformation gain significant advantages over their competitors, while those that struggle with it often find themselves falling behind in their markets.

1.3.3 Real-World Applications

Business analytics manifest in countless ways throughout the economy, often in forms that directly affect your daily experience as a consumer. When you shop online and see product recommendations based on your browsing history, you are experiencing the results of sophisticated analytics that predict what you might want to buy. When you receive a discount offer from a retailer shortly after visiting their website, you see targeted marketing based on analytical models that predict your likelihood of making a purchase.

The transportation industry provides another clear example of analytics in action. Ride-sharing services like Uber and Lyft use complex algorithms to match drivers with passengers, optimize routes, and adjust pricing based on supply and demand. These systems analyze real-time data about traffic conditions, driver locations, passenger requests, and historical patterns to make thousands of decisions every minute. The result is a service that can efficiently connect riders with drivers while maximizing utilization of available vehicles.

Even traditional industries have been transformed by analytics. Farmers now use data from satellites, weather stations, and soil sensors to optimize planting schedules, irrigation, and fertilizer applications. Manufacturers analyze production data to predict equipment failures before they occur, reducing downtime and maintenance costs. Healthcare providers use patient data to identify treatment protocols that produce the best outcomes while minimizing costs and side effects.

These examples illustrate how business analytics has moved beyond simple reporting to become a fundamental tool for operational excellence and competitive advantage. Companies that master these capabilities can respond more quickly to changing market conditions, serve their customers more effectively, and operate more efficiently than their competitors.

1.4 The Four Types of Business Analytics

Business analytics can be categorized into four distinct types, each serving different purposes and answering different questions. These types represent increasing levels of sophistication and value creation, building upon each other to provide comprehensive insights for decision-making. Understanding these categories helps clarify how businesses use data and what kinds of insights each approach can provide.

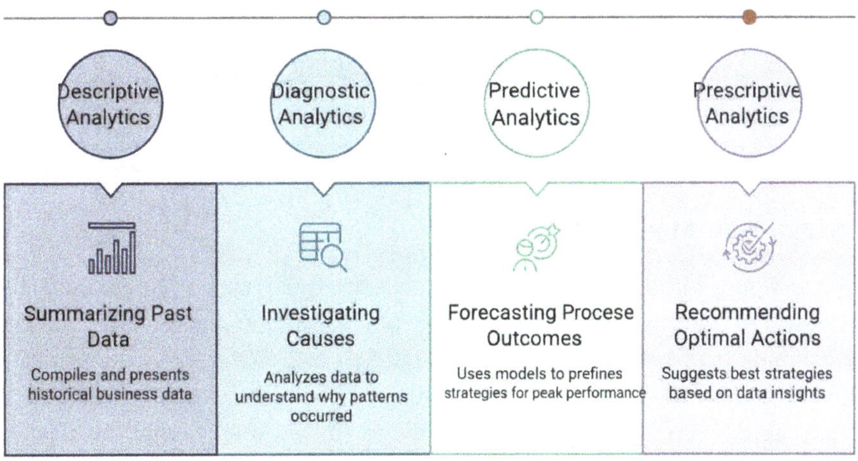

1.4.1 Descriptive Analytics

Descriptive analytics forms the foundation of all analytical work by summarizing historical data to provide clear pictures of past performance. This type of analysis answers the fundamental question of what happened during a specific period or in response to events. While it might seem basic compared to more advanced analytical techniques, descriptive analytics remains essential because it establishes the factual foundation upon which all other analysis builds.

Consider how a retail store might use descriptive analytics to understand their performance. At the end of each month, managers review sales reports that show total revenue, number of transactions, average purchase amounts, and best-selling products. These reports provide clear, factual summaries of what occurred during the month, allowing managers to understand their current position and identify areas that warrant further investigation.

The power of descriptive analytics lies in its ability to transform large volumes of raw data into understandable summaries. A grocery store might process thousands of individual transactions each day, but descriptive analytics can summarize this information to show daily sales totals, peak shopping hours, popular product categories, and seasonal trends. This summarized information becomes the starting point for understanding business performance and identifying opportunities for improvement.

Modern businesses use sophisticated tools to create descriptive analytics that go far beyond simple reports. Interactive dashboards allow managers to explore their data from multiple perspectives, drilling down from high-level summaries to detailed information about specific products, customers, or time periods. These tools make it possible for non-technical users to access and understand complex data without requiring advanced analytical skills.

However, descriptive analytics has important limitations that businesses must understand. While it can clearly show what happened, it provides no insight into why events occurred or what might happen in the future. A descriptive analysis might reveal that customer satisfaction scores declined in the third quarter, but it cannot explain whether this was due to product quality issues, service problems, competitive pressures, or external factors like economic conditions.

1.4.2 Diagnostic Analytics

Diagnostic analytics builds upon descriptive analytics by investigating the underlying causes of observed patterns and trends. This type of analysis answers the crucial question of why something happened, using various techniques to uncover the relationships and factors that drive business outcomes. Diagnostic analytics represents a significant step forward in analytical sophistication because it moves beyond simple reporting to provide explanations that can guide corrective actions.

The process of diagnostic analytics often begins with observations from descriptive analysis that raise questions or concerns. For example, a subscription-based service might notice from their descriptive analytics that customer cancellations increased by twenty percent last quarter. Diagnostic analytics would then investigate potential causes of this increase by examining various factors that might influence customer retention.

The investigation might reveal that cancellations were concentrated among customers who had experienced technical problems with the service, or among those who had not used certain features within their first month of subscription. By identifying these patterns, the company can understand the root causes of increased cancellations and develop targeted strategies to address them.

Diagnostic analytics employs various techniques to uncover these causal relationships.

Correlation analysis can identify factors that tend to change together, while segmentation analysis can reveal how different groups of customers or products behave differently. Time-series analysis can show how events unfold over time and identify potential trigger points for observed changes.

A restaurant chain might use diagnostic analytics to understand why some locations consistently outperform others. The analysis might examine factors such as local demographics, competition, store layout, staffing levels, and management practices. By identifying the characteristics that distinguish high-performing locations from average ones, the company can develop strategies to improve performance across their entire network.

The value of diagnostic analytics extends beyond problem-solving to opportunity identification. By understanding what drives positive outcomes, businesses can replicate successful strategies and avoid repeating mistakes. This type of analysis helps companies move from reactive problem-solving to proactive management based on understanding the underlying drivers of their performance.

1.4.3 Predictive Analytics

Predictive analytics represents a fundamental shift from analyzing the past to anticipating the future. This type of analysis uses historical data and statistical techniques to forecast what is likely to happen under various conditions. By providing insights into future trends and outcomes, predictive analytics enable businesses to make proactive decisions rather than simply reacting to events after they occur.

The foundation of predictive analytics lies in the assumption that patterns observed in historical data will continue, at least to some degree. A clothing retailer might analyze several years of sales data to identify seasonal patterns, then use these patterns to predict demand for different types of clothing in upcoming seasons. This forecast helps them make better decisions about inventory purchases, staffing levels, and marketing campaigns.

Netflix provides an excellent example of predictive analytics in action. The company analyzes viewing patterns of millions of subscribers to predict which shows and movies individual users are likely to enjoy. These predictions drive their recommendation system, which influences approximately eighty percent of the content that subscribers watch. By accurately predicting user preferences, Netflix can improve customer satisfaction while also optimizing their content acquisition and production investments.

Predictive analytics encompasses a wide range of techniques, from simple trend extrapolation to sophisticated machine learning algorithms. Time series forecasting might predict next quarter's sales based on historical patterns and seasonal trends. Customer lifetime value models estimate the total revenue that new customers will generate over their entire relationship with the company. Churn prediction models identify customers who are at risk of canceling their subscriptions, allowing companies to intervene with retention offers.

The retail industry demonstrates the practical value of predictive analytics through demand forecasting. Major retailers like Walmart use predictive models to anticipate demand for thousands of products across thousands of locations. These forecasts help them optimize inventory levels, reduce stock-outs and overstock situations, and improve customer satisfaction while minimizing costs.

However, predictive analytics require careful validation and ongoing monitoring to remain effective. Models trained on historical data may become less accurate as business conditions change or as the relationships between variables evolve over time. The COVID-19 pandemic provided a dramatic example of this challenge, as consumer behavior shifted so rapidly that many existing predictive models became obsolete almost overnight.

1.4.4 Prescriptive Analytics

Prescriptive analytics represents the most advanced form of business analytics, combining predictive capabilities with optimization techniques to recommend specific actions that will achieve desired outcomes. This type of analysis answers the ultimate question of what should be done, providing not just forecasts of what might happen, but specific guidance on how to influence those outcomes in favorable ways.

The sophistication of prescriptive analytics reflects the complexity of real business decisions, which often involve multiple objectives, constraints, and trade-offs. A delivery company like FedEx must simultaneously optimize routes to minimize fuel costs, meet customer delivery time requirements, comply with driver work hour regulations, and maintain service quality across their network. Prescriptive analytics can consider all these factors simultaneously and recommend specific actions that best balance competing objectives.

Ride-sharing companies provide compelling examples of prescriptive analytics in everyday use. These services must continuously make decisions about pricing, driver positioning, and route optimization based on real-time conditions. Their algorithms analyze current demand patterns, driver availability, traffic conditions, and historical data to recommend specific actions such as surge pricing in high-demand areas or incentives to attract drivers to underserved locations.

The airline industry has long been a leader in prescriptive analytics through revenue management systems that optimize seat pricing and availability. These systems consider factors such as historical booking patterns, current reservation levels, seasonal trends, competitive pricing, and remaining time until departure to recommend specific prices for each fare class on each flight. The goal is to maximize revenue by selling the right seats to the right customers at the right prices.

Prescriptive analytics often incorporates techniques from operations research, including linear programming, simulation modeling, and optimization algorithms. These mathematical approaches can handle complex problems with thousands of variables and constraints, finding optimal solutions that would be impossible to identify through manual analysis.

However, implementing prescriptive analytics successfully requires significant organizational capabilities beyond just technical tools. Companies must have high-quality data, sophisticated analytical skills, and strong processes for acting on analytical recommendations. They must also be prepared to measure the results of their actions and continuously refine their models based on observed outcomes. Without this organizational commitment, even the most sophisticated prescriptive models will fail to create value.

1.5 Analytics in Companies You Know

Understanding how familiar companies use business analytics helps illustrate these concepts in concrete terms and demonstrates the practical value that analytics can create. The following examples show how businesses you interact with regularly have built their success around sophisticated use of data and analytical insights.

1.5.1 Netflix: Personalization Through Data

Netflix has built its entire business model around the systematic use of data to understand and serve customer preferences. The company collects detailed information about every aspect of user behavior on their platform, from what shows people watch and for how long, to when they pause or rewind content, what devices they use, and what time of day they typically watch. This comprehensive data collection enables Netflix to create highly personalized experiences for each of their over 230 million subscribers worldwide.

The company's recommendation system represents one of the most sophisticated applications of predictive analytics in consumer services. Netflix analyzes viewing patterns across their entire subscriber base to identify similarities between users and predict what content each person might enjoy. These predictions drive the personalized recommendations that appear on each user's homepage, influencing approximately eighty percent of what people watch on the platform.

Beyond individual recommendations, Netflix uses analytics to make fundamental business decisions about content creation and acquisition. The company's decision to produce original series like ”House of Cards” was based on analytical insights showing that their subscribers enjoyed political dramas, films starring Kevin Spacey, and content directed by David Fincher. By combining these preferences, Netflix predicted that a political drama starring Kevin Spacey and directed by David Fincher would be successful with their audience.

Netflix also uses analytics to optimize the presentation of their content. The company tests different thumbnail images for the same show or movie to determine which images generate the highest click-through rates from different types of users. They have discovered that the most effective thumbnail images vary significantly based on user preferences and viewing history, leading them to show different images to different users for the same content.

The company's approach to content release demonstrates prescriptive analytics in action. Netflix's decision to release entire seasons of original series simultaneously, rather than following the traditional weekly episode format, was based on analytical insights showing that their subscribers preferred to binge-watch content. This data-driven approach to content distribution has influenced viewing habits across the entire entertainment industry.

1.5.2 Amazon: Analytics Across the Business

Amazon has integrated analytics into virtually every aspect of their operations, from customer-facing features like product recommendations to behind-the-scenes processes like inventory management and logistics optimization. The company's success demonstrates how comprehensive use of analytics can create competitive advantages across multiple dimensions of business performance.

The most visible application of Amazon's analytics capabilities is their product recommendation system. When you visit Amazon's website, you see personalized suggestions based on your browsing history, previous purchases, items in your shopping cart, and the behavior of customers with similar preferences. These recommendations appear throughout the shopping experience, from the homepage to product pages to the checkout process, and they drive approximately thirty-five percent of Amazon's revenue.

Amazon's inventory management system represents one of the most sophisticated applications of predictive analytics in retail. The company must predict demand for millions of products across hundreds of fulfillment centers, considering factors such as seasonal trends, promotional activities, regional preferences, and supply chain constraints. Their algorithms continuously analyze sales patterns and adjust inventory levels to minimize both stockouts and excess inventory while ensuring fast delivery to customers.

The company's pricing strategy demonstrates real-time prescriptive analytics at massive scale. Amazon's algorithms continuously monitor competitor prices, inventory levels, demand patterns, and profit margins to automatically adjust prices throughout the day. This dynamic pricing approach allows Amazon to remain competitive while optimizing profitability across their vast product catalog.

Amazon's logistics network showcases analytics applied to complex operational challenges. The company uses sophisticated algorithms to determine which fulfillment center should ship each order, considering factors such as inventory availability, shipping costs, delivery time requirements, and capacity constraints. These decisions are made automatically for millions of orders each day, optimizing the entire network for cost and service performance.

The development of Amazon Web Services (AWS) illustrates how analytics capabilities can create entirely new business opportunities. Amazon's experience managing their own massive computing infrastructure led them to offer similar services to other companies, creating a business that now generates billions in revenue and serves millions of customers worldwide.

1.5.3 Starbucks: Analytics in Retail Operations

Starbucks demonstrates how traditional retail businesses can use analytics to optimize operations and enhance customer experiences. The company collects data from multiple sources, including point-of-sale systems, mobile app usage, loyalty program participation, and external factors like weather and local events, to make better decisions about everything from menu offerings to store locations.

The company's approach to menu optimization illustrates descriptive and diagnostic analytics working together. Starbucks analyzes sales data to understand which beverages sell best at different times of day, seasons of the year, and geographic locations. They have discovered that iced beverage sales correlate strongly with temperature and weather conditions, while hot beverage preferences vary by region and season. This analysis helps them optimize their menu offerings and promotional activities to match customer preferences.

Starbucks uses predictive analytics for staffing decisions, analyzing historical sales patterns, local events, weather forecasts, and other factors to predict customer traffic at each location. These forecasts help store managers schedule appropriate staffing levels to maintain service quality while controlling labor costs. The company has found that accurate staffing predictions significantly impact both customer satisfaction and operational efficiency.

The Starbucks mobile app demonstrates how analytics can enhance customer experiences while generating valuable business insights. The app tracks customer preferences, purchase history, and location data to provide personalized offers and recommendations. Customers who frequently order the same beverage might receive offers for complementary food items, while those who visit multiple locations might get promotions for stores along their regular routes.

Store location decisions at Starbucks involve sophisticated analytical models that consider demographic data, foot traffic patterns, competition analysis, and real estate costs. The company uses these models to identify optimal locations for new stores and to predict the sales potential of each location. This analytical approach to expansion has helped Starbucks maintain profitability while growing to over 30,000 locations worldwide.

The company's loyalty program generates valuable data that enables more sophisticated customer analytics. By tracking individual customer behavior over time, Starbucks can identify patterns such as frequency of visits, preferred products, price sensitivity, and response to promotional offers. This information enables highly targeted marketing campaigns and personalized customer experiences that increase loyalty and spending.

1.5.4 Walmart: Analytics at Scale

Walmart's use of analytics demonstrates how traditional retailers can leverage data to compete effectively in the modern marketplace. As the world's largest retailer, Walmart processes enormous volumes of data from thousands of stores, millions of customers, and complex supply chain operations. The company's analytical capabilities enable them to optimize operations at a scale that would be impossible to manage through traditional methods.

The company's inventory management system processes over 2.5 petabytes of data every hour, analyzing sales patterns, supply chain information, weather forecasts, and local events to optimize inventory levels across their network. This system helps ensure that popular items remain in stock while minimizing excess inventory that ties up capital and storage space. The scale of this operation requires sophisticated algorithms that can make millions of inventory decisions automatically.

Walmart uses predictive analytics to anticipate demand fluctuations caused by external events. The company has developed models that predict how weather events, holidays, local emergencies, and economic conditions will affect demand for different products in different regions. For example, their algorithms can predict increased demand for batteries and flashlights before hurricanes make landfall, enabling them to position inventory appropriately.

The company's supply chain optimization demonstrates prescriptive analytics applied to complex logistical challenges. Walmart's systems continuously optimize transportation routes, warehouse operations, and supplier relationships to minimize costs while maintaining service levels. These optimizations consider factors such as fuel costs, driver availability, warehouse capacity, and delivery time requirements across their entire network.

Walmart's approach to pricing illustrates how analytics can support competitive strategy. The company uses sophisticated algorithms to monitor competitor prices, analyze price elasticity for different products, and optimize pricing to maintain their position as a low-cost leader while preserving profitability. This dynamic approach to pricing requires continuous analysis of market conditions and competitive responses.

The company's expansion into e-commerce has required new analytical capabilities to compete with online retailers like Amazon. Walmart has developed recommendation systems, personalization algorithms, and digital marketing optimization tools to enhance their online customer experience. These capabilities complement their physical store network and create integrated shopping experiences that leverage both online and offline data.

1.6 Role of Artificial Intelligence in Business Analytics

Artificial intelligence has fundamentally transformed how businesses approach analytics, enabling them to process vastly larger amounts of data, identify more complex patterns, and make decisions at speeds that would be impossible for human analysts alone. Understanding AI's role in business analytics helps clarify both the opportunities and limitations of these powerful technologies.

1.6.1 Understanding AI in Business Context

Artificial intelligence in business analytics refers to computer systems that can learn from data, identify patterns, and make predictions or recommendations without being explicitly programmed for every possible situation. These systems can process enormous amounts of information simultaneously, operate continuously without fatigue, and identify subtle relationships in data that human analysts might miss.

The practical impact of AI becomes clear when we consider the scale of modern business operations. A large e-commerce company might process millions of customer interactions each day, generating data about browsing behavior, purchase patterns, customer service contacts, and product reviews. Human analysts could never process all this information in real-time, but AI systems can analyze it continuously and provide immediate insights and recommendations.

AI systems excel at pattern recognition, which makes them particularly valuable for business analytics. They can identify complex relationships between variables that might not be obvious to human observers. For example, an AI system might discover that customers who purchase certain combinations of products are more likely to return items, or that specific sequences of website interactions predict higher conversion rates.

However, AI systems also have important limitations that businesses must understand. They typically require large amounts of high-quality data to function effectively, and their performance can degrade if the underlying patterns in the data change over time. AI systems also struggle with situations that fall outside their training data and may have difficulty explaining their decisions in ways that humans can easily understand.

1.6.2 AI Applications in Everyday Business

Social media platforms provide familiar examples of AI analytics in action. When you open Facebook, Instagram, or TikTok, AI algorithms analyze your past behavior, current context, and the behavior of similar users to determine which posts to show you. These systems process millions of pieces of content and user interactions to create personalized feeds that maximize engagement and satisfaction.

Online shopping experiences demonstrate AI's ability to enhance customer service and increase sales. When you browse an e-commerce website, AI systems track your behavior and use it to personalize your experience in real-time. They might highlight products like ones you've viewed, adjust the layout of the website based on your preferences, or determine the optimal time to show you promotional offers.

Customer service chatbots illustrate how AI can automate routine interactions while providing valuable data for business improvement. These systems can handle common customer questions, process simple transactions, and escalate complex issues to human agents. They also generate data about customer concerns and preferences that businesses can use to improve their products and services.

Fraud detection systems in banking and e-commerce demonstrate AI's ability to identify unusual patterns in large datasets. These systems analyze millions of transactions to identify potentially fraudulent activity based on factors such as transaction amounts, locations, timing, and merchant types. They can flag suspicious transactions for human review while allowing normal transactions to proceed without delay.

1.6.3 Benefits and Capabilities of AI Analytics

A cartoon of a robot with a brain above it talking at a desk to men with computers

AI systems provide several key advantages that make them valuable for business analytics. Their ability to process large volumes of data quickly enables real-time analysis and decision-making that would be impossible with traditional methods. A ride-sharing company can use AI to optimize pricing and driver allocation across an entire city in real-time, responding to changing conditions as they occur.

The pattern recognition capabilities of AI systems allow them to identify complex relationships that might not be apparent through traditional analytical methods. Machine learning algorithms can discover that customer satisfaction is influenced by subtle combinations of factors that human analysts might not consider together, leading to more effective improvement strategies.

AI systems can operate continuously without breaks, providing consistent monitoring and analysis around the clock. This capability is particularly valuable for businesses that operate globally or need to respond quickly to changing conditions. An e-commerce company can use AI to continuously optimize their website performance and product recommendations based on real-time customer behavior.

The scalability of AI systems allows businesses to apply sophisticated analytics across their entire operations without proportional increases in analytical staff. A retail chain can use the same AI algorithms to optimize inventory and pricing across thousands of locations, achieving consistency and efficiency that would be difficult to maintain with manual processes.

1.6.4 Limitations and Considerations

Despite their capabilities, AI systems have important limitations that businesses must consider when implementing them. Data quality remains a fundamental concern because AI systems can only be as good as the data they are trained on. Poor quality data can lead to biased or inaccurate models that make poor recommendations and potentially harm business performance.

The interpretability of AI decisions varies significantly across different types of systems. Simple models may provide clear explanations for their recommendations, while complex deep learning systems may function as "black boxes" that provide accurate results without clear explanations of their reasoning. This lack of transparency can be problematic in regulated industries or situations where understanding the reasoning behind decisions is important.

AI systems can perpetuate or amplify biases present in their training data. If historical data reflects discriminatory practices or unrepresentative samples, AI systems trained on this data may continue these biases in their recommendations. Businesses must actively monitor their AI systems for bias and implement corrective measures when necessary.

The dynamic nature of business environments means that AI models may become less accurate over time as conditions change. Models trained on historical data may not perform well when market conditions, customer preferences, or competitive landscapes shift significantly. Successful AI implementations require ongoing monitoring and model updating to maintain effectiveness.

1.6.5 The Future of AI in Business

The integration of AI into business analytics continues to evolve rapidly, with new capabilities and applications emerging regularly. Natural language processing is making it easier for non-technical users to interact with analytical systems, while computer vision is enabling analysis of visual data such as images and videos.

The democratization of AI tools is making sophisticated analytics accessible to smaller businesses that previously could not afford such capabilities. Cloud-based AI services allow companies to access powerful analytical tools without significant upfront investments in technology infrastructure or specialized staff.

However, the successful adoption of AI in business analytics requires more than just technology. Companies must develop organizational capabilities to work effectively with AI systems, including data management processes, analytical skills, and change management practices. They must also address ethical considerations around data privacy, algorithmic bias, and the impact of automation on employment.

The most successful applications of AI in business analytics will likely involve human-AI collaboration, where AI systems handle data processing and pattern identification while humans provide context, judgment, and strategic direction. This partnership approach leverages the strengths of both human and artificial intelligence to create more effective analytical capabilities than either could achieve alone.

1.7 Conclusion

This module has introduced the fundamentals of business analytics, showing how data shapes modern business and influences daily life as a consumer. Analytics is not just a technical skill but a systematic approach to decision-making that creates value across industries. The four types of analytics—descriptive, diagnostic, predictive, and prescriptive—build on one another to provide deeper insights and actionable recommendations. Real-world examples from companies like Netflix, Amazon, Starbucks, and Walmart demonstrate how effective use of data drives competitive advantage, improves customer experiences, and enhances operational efficiency.

Artificial intelligence expands analytics capabilities by processing large data sets and identifying complex patterns, but human judgment remains essential in interpreting results and making strategic decisions. Analytics literacy also helps you navigate the business world as a consumer, make informed choices about privacy, and evaluate marketing and pricing strategies. The principles covered here provide a foundation for advanced study and immediate application in personal, academic, and professional decisions. Combining analytical thinking with human judgment enables better decision-making and value creation, and mastering these basics will serve you throughout your career.

1.8 Key Terms

Business Analytics: The systematic use of data and analysis to inform business decisions and create value.

Descriptive Analytics: Summarizes historical data to show what happened in the past.

Diagnostic Analytics: Investigates the reasons behind past outcomes to answer why events occurred.

Predictive Analytics: Uses historical data to forecast future outcomes and trends.

Prescriptive Analytics: Recommends actions to achieve desired outcomes based on predictive insights.

Artificial Intelligence (AI): Technology that enables machines to process data, recognize patterns, and make decisions.

Pattern Recognition: The ability to identify trends, relationships, or anomalies in data.

Data-Driven Decision Making: Making decisions based on evidence from data rather than intuition alone.

Analytics Literacy: The ability to understand, interpret, and apply analytical insights effectively.

Ethical Data Use: Using data responsibly, considering fairness, privacy, and potential biases in analysis.

1.9 Review Questions

1. What distinguishes the four types of analytics from one another?
2. How do companies like Netflix or Amazon use analytics to gain a competitive advantage?
3. What are the benefits and limitations of AI in business analytics?
4. How can analytical thinking improve decision-making in personal life?
5. Why is analytics literacy becoming increasingly important across all career paths?
6. How does understanding analytics help you navigate your role as a consumer?
7. What ethical considerations arise from the use of AI and data-driven decision-making?

1.10 References

[1] Verified Market Research. (2024). *Business Analytics Market Size & Forecast.* https://www.verifiedmarketresearch.com/product/global-business-analytics-market-size-and-forecast/

[2] DataCamp. (2024). *The State of Data & AI Literacy Report 2024.* https://www.datacamp.com/blog/introducing-the-state-of-data-and-ai-literacy-report-2024

[3] Analytics8. (2024). *Four Types of Analytics and Their Differences.* https://www.analytics8.com/blog/what-are-the-four-types-of-analytics-and-how-do-you-use-them/

Chapter 2

Descriptive Analytics

2.1 Learning Outcomes

2-1. Recognize key performance indicators (KPIs) and understand how dashboards communicate business performance

2-2. Identify trends, patterns, and changes in business data over time

2-3. Understand how businesses create reports and visualizations to share information

2-4. Recognize how artificial intelligence helps businesses analyze and summarize data

2.2 Introduction

Imagine walking into the headquarters of a major retail chain during their Monday morning executive briefing. On the wall-mounted displays, colorful dashboards show

weekend sales performance across 2,000 stores, customer traffic patterns, inventory levels, and social media sentiment. Within minutes, executives can see that weekend sales exceeded projections by 8%, but customer satisfaction scores in the Northeast region dropped by 12 points, and inventory turnover for winter apparel is lagging seasonal expectations.

This scenario illustrates descriptive analytics in action—the systematic process of examining historical data to understand what happened in your business. While it might seem straightforward, descriptive analytics forms the foundation upon which all other analytical activities are built. You cannot predict the future or make recommendations about what to do next without first understanding the past and present state of your business.

Think of descriptive analytics like looking in your rearview mirror while driving. It shows you where you've been and what has happened, which is essential information for understanding your current situation. Just as you need to know where you've been to navigate effectively, businesses need to understand their past performance to make good decisions about the future.

Descriptive analytics accounts for approximately 80% of all analytical activities in most organizations, making it the most widely used form of business analytics. This prevalence reflects both its accessibility and its fundamental importance. Unlike predictive or prescriptive analytics, which require sophisticated computer models, descriptive analytics can be performed with basic tools and knowledge, making it the entry point for most organizations beginning their analytics journey.

However, the apparent simplicity of descriptive analytics can be deceiving. The difference between basic reporting and insightful descriptive analytics lies in the ability to transform raw data into meaningful information that drives decision-making. Consider two approaches to analyzing customer data: a basic report might show that customer complaints increased by 15% last quarter, while sophisticated descriptive analytics would reveal that complaints spiked specifically among customers aged 25-34 in urban markets, primarily related to mobile app functionality, with the highest concentration occurring during evening hours.

The business value of effective descriptive analytics is substantial. Organizations that excel at descriptive analytics report 15-20% improvements in operational efficiency and 10-15% reductions in costs compared to those with basic reporting capabilities. This value creation stems from the ability to identify patterns, spot unusual occurrences, and understand what drives business performance.

Modern descriptive analytics has been transformed by advances in data visualization, automated reporting, and artificial intelligence. What once required teams of analysts working with spreadsheets can now be accomplished through interactive dashboards that update in real-time. AI-powered tools can automatically identify significant patterns in data and generate written summaries that explain key findings in plain language.

Throughout this module, we will explore the essential components of descriptive analytics, from understanding key performance indicators and dashboards to recognizing trends and patterns in business data. We will examine how businesses create compelling visualizations that tell clear stories with data and understand how AI is revolutionizing the speed and accessibility of descriptive analytics. Whether you are looking at sales performance for a small business or operational metrics for a large corporation, these concepts will help you understand how data gets transformed into insights that drive better business decisions.

2.3 Key Performance Indicators and Dashboards

2.3.1 Understanding What KPIs Really Are

Key Performance Indicators, commonly called KPIs, represent the vital signs of a business—the specific measurements that best show whether an organization is achieving its goals. However, not all numbers qualify as KPIs. The distinction between general statistics and true KPIs lies in their direct connection to business outcomes and their ability to help people make decisions.

Think of KPIs like the dashboard in your car. Your car collects hundreds of pieces of information—engine temperature, oil pressure, fuel level, speed, RPM, and many others. But your dashboard only shows you the most important ones that you need to drive safely and effectively. Similarly, businesses collect enormous amounts of data, but KPIs are the most important measurements that help managers run the business effectively.

Effective KPIs share several important characteristics. They are directly connected to business goals, they can be measured with numbers, they can be influenced by actions the organization can take, and they provide timely information that enables quick responses to problems or opportunities. A well-designed KPI system creates a clear connection between daily work activities and long-term business success.

Consider how KPIs have evolved in the retail industry over the past few decades. Traditional retailers focused primarily on sales revenue and profit margins—basically, how much money they made and how much they kept after expenses. Modern retailers track a much broader set of KPIs including customer lifetime value (how much a customer will spend over their entire relationship with the store), net promoter score (how likely customers are to recommend the store to friends), inventory turnover by category (how quickly different types of products sell), and social media sentiment (what people are saying about the store online).

This expansion reflects the increasing complexity of modern business and the recognition that financial outcomes are driven by underlying operational and customer experience factors. A store might have good sales this month, but if customer satisfaction is declining and inventory is piling up, those could be warning signs of future problems.

The selection of appropriate KPIs requires careful consideration of your business model, industry, and strategic priorities. A subscription-based software company like Netflix might prioritize monthly recurring revenue (predictable income from subscriptions), customer churn rate (how many people cancel each month), and customer acquisition cost (how much it costs to get a new subscriber). Meanwhile, a manufacturing company might focus on overall equipment effectiveness (how well machines are running), defect rates (how many products have problems), and on-time delivery performance (whether products reach customers when promised).

2.3.2 How KPIs Work Together: The Hierarchy System

Effective KPI systems are organized like a pyramid, with high-level strategic KPIs at the top cascading down to more detailed tactical and operational metrics. This hierarchy ensures that daily activities connect to long-term objectives while providing appropriate levels of detail for different people in the organization.

Strategic KPIs sit at the top of the pyramid and focus on overall business performance. These are typically reviewed by senior executives on a monthly or quarterly basis. Examples might include revenue growth rate, market share, return on investment, and overall customer satisfaction scores. Strategic KPIs provide a high-level view of business health but offer limited guidance for specific improvements that individual employees can make.

Tactical KPIs occupy the middle level and bridge the gap between strategic objectives and daily activities. These metrics are typically reviewed by middle management on a weekly or monthly basis and focus on specific functional areas. For a marketing organization, tactical KPIs might include lead generation rates (how many potential customers they identify), conversion rates by channel (what percentage of potential customers actually buy through different marketing approaches), cost per acquisition (how much it costs to get each new customer), and campaign return on investment (how much revenue each marketing campaign generates compared to its cost).

Operational KPIs focus on specific processes and activities and are typically monitored daily or even hourly. These metrics enable front-line managers and employees to make real-time adjustments to their work. In a customer service organization, operational KPIs might include average response time (how long customers wait for help), first-call resolution rate (what percentage of problems get solved on the first phone call), and customer satisfaction scores by individual representative.

The power of hierarchical KPI systems lies in their ability to connect daily work to strategic outcomes. When a customer service representative sees that their first-call resolution rate is below target, they understand how this impacts overall customer satisfaction scores, which in turn affects customer retention and ultimately revenue growth. This connection helps employees understand why their individual performance matters to the bigger picture.

2.3.3 Understanding Business Dashboards

Dashboards serve as the primary interface between data and decision-makers, transforming complex datasets into visual stories that enable quick understanding and action. Think of a business dashboard like the instrument panel in an airplane cockpit—it presents the most critical information in a format that allows for quick assessment and immediate action when needed.

However, effective dashboard design requires more than simply putting charts on a screen. It demands careful consideration of who will use the dashboard, what decisions they need to make, and how they process visual information. A dashboard designed for a CEO needs to present different information and use different formatting than one designed for a front-line supervisor.

The most fundamental principle of dashboard design is understanding your audience and their decision-making context. Executive dashboards typically focus on high-level trends and exception reporting—they highlight when things are going unusually well or poorly so that executives can focus their attention appropriately. Operational dashboards, on the other hand, provide detailed, real-time information about specific processes so that supervisors can make immediate adjustments when problems arise.

Visual hierarchy plays a crucial role in effective dashboard design. The human eye follows predictable patterns when scanning visual information, typically starting at the top-left and moving in a Z-pattern across the screen. Effective dashboards place the most important information in these high-attention areas and use visual cues such as size, color, and positioning to guide the viewer's attention to critical insights.

Color usage in dashboards requires particular attention. While color can be a powerful tool for highlighting important information and creating visual appeal, it can also create confusion if used inconsistently. Effective dashboards establish clear color conventions—such as red for problems or negative performance, green for good performance, and yellow for caution—and apply these consistently throughout the interface.

The principle of progressive disclosure suggests that dashboards should present information at multiple levels of detail, allowing users to start with summary views and then drill down to detailed analysis as needed. A sales dashboard might show overall revenue performance at the top level, with the ability to click through to see regional performance, then individual store performance, then specific product performance.

2.3.4 A Real Dashboard Example

To illustrate these concepts, let's examine a practical example using monthly sales data from a hypothetical retail business. The KPIs selected for this example focus on revenue performance and goal achievement, which are fundamental concerns for most businesses.

The dashboard tracks four key metrics: Total Sales (the overall revenue generated during the analysis period), Average Monthly Sales (a baseline for typical performance), Sales Growth Rate (measuring improvement or decline over time), and Sales Variance from Target (evaluating performance relative to predetermined goals). Together, these KPIs provide insight into overall performance level, performance trends, and alignment with business targets.

Here's the monthly sales data that forms the foundation of our dashboard:

Month	Sales	Target	Variance
2024-01	95	105	-10
2024-02	102	105	-3
2024-03	110	105	5
2024-04	108	105	3
2024-05	115	105	10
2024-06	123	105	18

From this data, we can calculate our key performance indicators:

KPI	Value
Total Sales	653
Average Monthly Sales	108.83
Overall Sales Growth Rate (%)	29.50

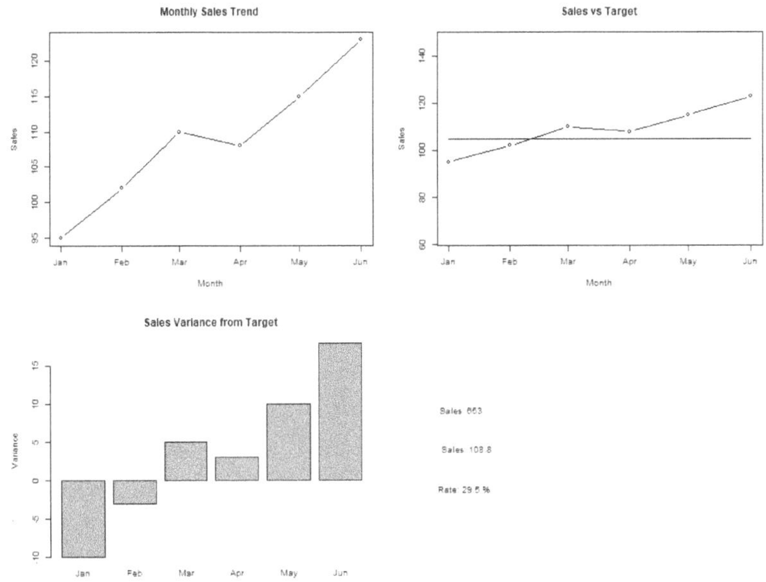

The accompanying dashboard presents four complementary views of performance. A sales trend plot illustrates changes over time, showing the upward trajectory from January through June. A comparison plot highlights differences between actual sales and targets, revealing that performance started below target but improved significantly over time. A variance chart emphasizes the magnitude and direction of deviations from goals, clearly showing the transition from negative to positive variances. Finally, a text panel summarizes key KPI values for quick reference.

This simple dashboard structure demonstrates how multiple KPIs can be integrated into a single, coherent view to support data-driven decision-making. Rather than looking at individual numbers in isolation, the dashboard tells a complete story about business performance, trends, and goal achievement.

2.4 Trends and Patterns in Business Data

2.4.1 What Trend Analysis Really Means

Trend analysis forms the backbone of descriptive analytics, enabling organizations to understand how their business metrics change over time. While the concept might seem straightforward—simply plotting data points across time periods—effective trend analysis requires understanding seasonal patterns, cyclical variations, and underlying business drivers that influence performance.

Think of trend analysis like tracking your grades throughout a semester. If you just looked at individual test scores, you might see that you got an 85 on one test and a 78 on another. But trend analysis would help you understand whether your performance is generally improving, declining, or staying stable over time. It would also help you identify patterns, like whether you tend to perform better on certain types of tests or during certain parts of the semester.

The foundation of trend analysis lies in distinguishing between different types of patterns in time-based data. Linear trends show consistent increases or decreases over time, such as steady revenue growth or declining customer satisfaction scores. Seasonal patterns repeat at regular intervals, such as retail sales spikes during holiday periods or ice cream sales increases during summer months. Cyclical patterns occur over longer, irregular periods and often reflect broader economic or industry cycles.

Consider how a subscription-based software company like Spotify might analyze customer cancellation trends. A basic trend analysis might show that monthly cancellation rates have increased from 2.1% to 2.8% over the past year. However, sophisticated trend analysis would break down this pattern to identify seasonal effects (cancellations typically spike at year-end as companies review their software subscriptions), cyclical patterns (cancellations increase during economic downturns when companies cut costs), and underlying trends (gradual increase in cancellations among specific customer segments who may be switching to competitors).

2.4.2 A Detailed Look at Sales Trends

To illustrate these concepts, let's examine a comprehensive trend analysis using 36 months of sales data. This analysis demonstrates how businesses can separate different components of their performance to understand what's really driving their results.

The following data shows how trend decomposition works, breaking down actual sales figures into their underlying components:

Month	Sales	12-Month MA	Trend	Seasonal	Remainder
2022-01	95.24	-	100.00	-4.76	0.00
2022-02	103.89	-	102.78	1.11	0.00
2022-03	118.65	-	105.56	13.09	0.00
2022-06	156.83	125.42	125.00	31.83	0.00
2022-12	189.32	145.23	150.00	39.32	0.00
2023-06	201.54	165.87	162.50	39.04	0.00
2023-12	225.71	185.34	175.00	50.71	0.00
2024-06	238.92	205.12	187.50	51.42	0.00
2024-12	262.43	225.67	200.00	62.43	0.00

This table reveals several important insights. First, there are clear seasonal patterns with December consistently showing the highest seasonal component (39-62 points above the underlying trend). Second, there's steady underlying growth from 100 to 200 over the 36-month period, representing a doubling of the baseline business performance.

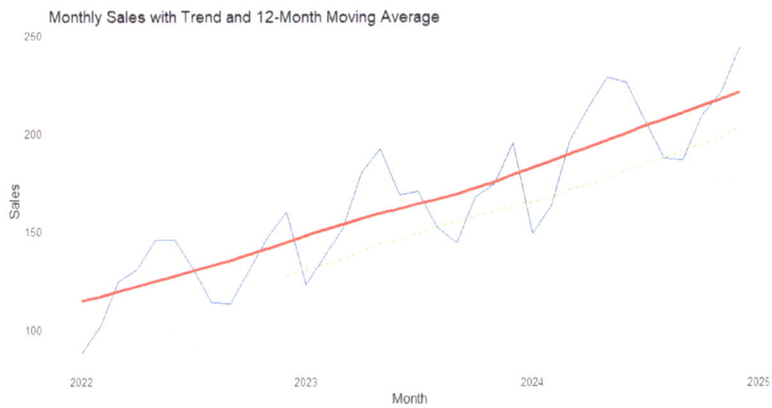

The choice of time periods for trend analysis significantly impacts the insights you can generate. Daily data provides detailed information but may be too noisy to identify meaningful patterns—like trying to understand your overall health by weighing yourself multiple times per day. Monthly data smooths out short-term fluctuations but may miss important weekly patterns. Annual data reveals long-term trends but obscures seasonal and cyclical variations.

The visualization above demonstrates this concept through a line graph showing three data series over the 36-month period from January 2022 to December 2024. The fluctuating blue line represents actual monthly sales data, showing both seasonal ups and downs and an overall upward trend. The straight red line displays the underlying trend component, demonstrating steady linear growth from approximately 100 to 200. The green dashed line shows the 12-month moving average, which smooths out seasonal variations to reveal the consistent growth pattern.

This chart clearly illustrates how seasonal effects create regular peaks and valleys around the underlying trend, with December consistently showing the highest values each year. Understanding these patterns helps businesses distinguish between temporary seasonal fluctuations and genuine changes in their underlying performance.

Moving averages represent one of the most powerful techniques for trend analysis. By calculating averages over rolling time periods, moving averages smooth out short-term fluctuations to reveal underlying trends. A 12-month moving average of sales data eliminates seasonal variations to show underlying growth or decline patterns. However, moving averages also introduce lag, meaning they may not quickly reflect recent changes in trends.

2.4.3 Advanced Techniques for Understanding Trends

Year-over-year comparisons provide valuable context for trend analysis by accounting for seasonal patterns. Comparing current month's performance to the same month in the previous year eliminates seasonal effects while highlighting underlying changes in business performance. For example, comparing December 2024 sales to December

2023 sales gives you a clearer picture of actual growth than comparing December 2024 to November 2024.

However, year-over-year comparisons can be misleading when unusual events occurred in the comparison period. If a major competitor went out of business in December 2023, then December 2024 sales might look artificially good compared to that unusual baseline.

Compound Annual Growth Rate (CAGR) calculations enable comparison of growth rates across different time periods and business metrics. CAGR smooths out year-to-year variations to show average annual growth rates, making it easier to compare the performance of different products, regions, or time periods. For example, a product line showing 15% CAGR over three years demonstrates stronger underlying growth than one showing 25% growth in year one followed by declines in subsequent years.

The concept of leading and lagging indicators adds sophistication to trend analysis. Leading indicators change before the metrics you're trying to understand, while lagging indicators change after. Website traffic might be a leading indicator for sales—if more people visit your website this month, you might see increased sales next month. Customer satisfaction scores might be lagging because they reflect the impact of changes you made in previous months. Understanding these relationships enables more proactive decision-making.

2.4.4 Understanding Variance Analysis

Variance analysis compares actual performance to planned or expected performance, providing insights into business execution and environmental changes. While trend analysis focuses on patterns over time, variance analysis focuses on differences between what you expected to happen and what happened at specific points in time.

Think of variance analysis like comparing your actual test score to what you expected to get. If you expected to score 90% but scored 85%, the variance analysis would help you understand whether this difference was due to the test being harder than expected, your preparation being insufficient, or other factors that affected your performance.

The foundation of effective variance analysis lies in establishing appropriate benchmarks for comparison. These benchmarks might include budgets (what you planned to achieve), forecasts (what you predicted would happen), prior period performance (how you did last year), or industry standards (how similar companies typically perform). The choice of benchmark significantly impacts on the insights generated and the actions that result from the analysis.

Budget variance analysis compares actual performance to budgeted expectations, revealing areas where execution exceeded or fell short of plans. A marketing department might budget $100,000 for digital advertising with an expected return of 500 new customers. If actual spending was $110,000 but generated 600 new customers, the analysis would reveal both unfavorable cost variance (spent more than planned) and favorable volume variance (got more customers than expected).

2.4.5 A Practical Variance Analysis Example

Let's examine how variance analysis works using actual versus budgeted sales performance over a 36-month period:

Table 2.4: Monthly Sales vs Budget Analysis

Month	Sales	Budget	Variance	Variance %	Status
2022-01	95.24	105.00	-9.76	-9.3	Unfavorable
2022-02	103.89	107.92	-4.03	-3.7	Unfavorable
2022-03	118.65	110.83	7.82	7.1	Favorable
2022-06	156.83	131.25	25.58	19.5	Favorable
2022-12	189.32	157.50	31.82	20.2	Favorable
2023-06	201.54	170.63	30.91	18.1	Favorable
2023-12	225.71	183.75	41.96	22.8	Favorable
2024-06	238.92	196.88	42.04	21.4	Favorable
2024-12	262.43	210.00	52.43	25.0	Favorable

This variance analysis shows initial unfavorable performance in early 2022, followed by consistently favorable variances, with performance improving significantly above budget expectations over time.

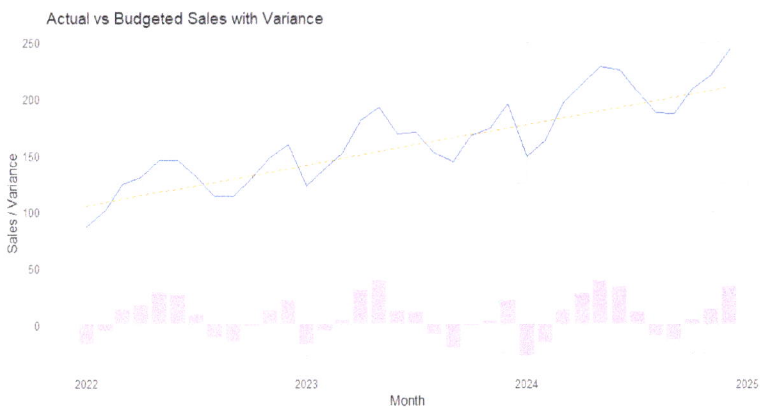

The combination chart above displays actual sales performance against budgeted expectations over the 36-month period. The blue line shows actual sales data with its characteristic seasonal patterns and growth trend, while the orange dashed line represents the budgeted sales, showing a more conservative linear growth projection. Purple bars indicate the variance between actual and budgeted performance, with negative bars below the baseline representing unfavorable variances (early 2022) and positive bars above representing favorable variances (majority of the period).

This visualization clearly demonstrates how actual performance exceeded budget expectations increasingly over time, with the largest favorable variances occurring during peak seasonal periods. This pattern suggests that the business not only met its goals but significantly outperformed them, particularly during high-demand periods.

Favorable and unfavorable variances require different analytical approaches. Favorable variances might indicate successful execution, favorable market conditions, or conservative planning. Unfavorable variances might reflect execution problems, adverse market conditions, or overly optimistic planning. The key insight lies not just in identifying variances but in understanding their underlying causes so that successful strategies can be repeated and problems can be addressed.

2.4.6 Understanding Ratio Analysis

Ratio analysis examines relationships between different business metrics, revealing insights about efficiency, profitability, and performance that cannot be understood by looking at individual numbers in isolation. Ratios provide context for absolute numbers and enable meaningful comparisons across time periods, business units, and companies.

Think of ratios like statistics in sports. A basketball player's total points scored tells you something, but their points per game tells you more about their consistent performance. Their shooting percentage tells you about their efficiency. Their assists-to-turnovers ratio tells you about their decision-making. Each ratio provides a different perspective on overall performance.

Profitability ratios examine the relationship between revenues and various cost categories. Gross profit margin (gross profit divided by revenue) reveals the efficiency of core business operations—how much money the company keeps from each dollar of sales after paying for the direct costs of producing their products or services. Operating profit margin (operating profit divided by revenue) shows the efficiency of overall business operations including overhead costs like rent, salaries, and marketing. Net profit margin (net profit divided by revenue) reflects the bottom-line profitability after all expenses, including taxes and interest payments.

2.4.7 Financial Ratios in Action

Let's examine how ratio analysis works using financial data from our hypothetical business:

Table 2.5: Ratios

Month	Gross Profit Margin	Operating Profit Margin	Net Profit Margin	Inventory Turnover	Current Ratio
2022-01	42.85	19.23	18.52	8.21	1.45
2022-06	44.12	20.15	19.87	8.67	1.52
2022-12	43.56	19.89	18.94	8.45	1.48
2023-06	45.23	21.34	20.12	9.12	1.58
2023-12	44.87	20.98	19.76	8.89	1.54
2024-06	46.15	22.11	21.45	9.34	1.62
2024-12	45.67	21.78	20.89	9.18	1.59

The ratio analysis demonstrates improving profitability margins over time, with gross profit margin increasing from 42.85% to 45.67%, and inventory turnover improving from 8.21 to 9.18, indicating enhanced operational efficiency.

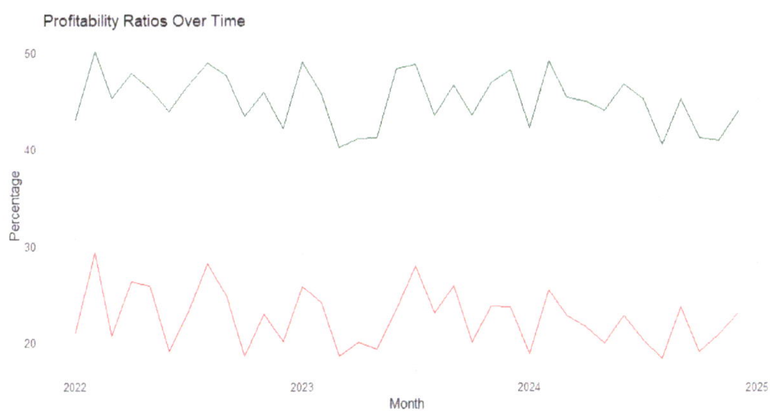

The dual-line chart tracking profitability ratios across the analysis period shows the dark green line representing gross profit margin, demonstrating steady improvement from approximately 43% to 46% with some seasonal fluctuation. The red line displays net profit margin, showing growth from about 18.5% to 21% over the period. Both lines show generally upward trends with periodic variations, indicating improving profitability performance and illustrating the consistent gap between gross and net margins, reflecting the impact of operating expenses on bottom-line profitability.

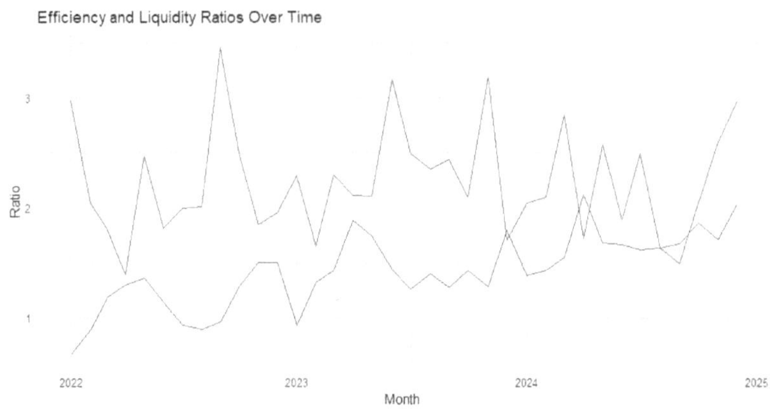

Efficiency ratios measure how effectively an organization uses its resources. Inventory turnover (cost of goods sold divided by average inventory) shows how quickly inventory is converted to sales—higher numbers generally indicate better performance because the company isn't tying up money in unsold products. Accounts receivable turnover (revenue divided by average accounts receivable) indicates how quickly customers pay their bills. Asset turnover (revenue divided by total assets) measures how efficiently assets generate revenue.

The chart displaying two operational ratios tracked monthly over the analysis period shows the lower blue line representing the inventory turnover ratio, which fluctuates between approximately 8 and 9.5, showing some variability over time with a modest upward tendency toward the end of the period, suggesting gradual improvement in inventory management efficiency. The upper purple line represents the current ratio, ranging from about 1.4 to 1.6, indicating relatively stable liquidity with some month-to-month variation but generally remaining above 1.0, which reflects an adequate ability to pay short-term debts.

Liquidity ratios assess an organization's ability to meet short-term obligations. Current ratio (current assets divided by current liabilities) measures the ability to pay short-term debts. A ratio above 1.0 indicates that the company has more current assets than current liabilities, which is generally considered healthy. Quick ratio (liquid assets divided by current liabilities) provides a more conservative measure by excluding inventory from current assets, focusing on the most liquid assets like cash and accounts receivable.

The power of ratio analysis lies in trend analysis and benchmarking. A current ratio of 2.0 might seem healthy, but if it has declined from 3.0 over the past year, it might indicate emerging liquidity concerns. Similarly, ratios gain meaning through comparison to industry benchmarks or competitor performance. A 15% net profit margin might be excellent in the grocery industry but poor in the software industry.

2.5 Business Reporting and Data Visualization

2.5.1 How Business Reporting Has Changed

Business reporting has undergone a fundamental transformation over the past decade, evolving from static, backward-looking documents to dynamic, interactive experiences that enable real-time decision-making. This evolution reflects changes in technology capabilities, user expectations, and the pace of business operations.

Traditional business reports were typically produced monthly or quarterly, distributed as printed documents or PDF files, and focused primarily on financial performance. Think of these like report cards that you might have received in school—they told you how you performed in the past, but by the time you received them, it was too late to change anything about that performance period. These reports served important record-keeping and compliance functions but provided limited value for day-to-day decision-making due to their delayed timing and static format.

Modern business reporting emphasizes real-time or near-real-time information delivery through interactive dashboards and automated alert systems. Rather than waiting for monthly reports, managers can access current performance information whenever they need it, much like checking your bank account balance on your phone app. This shift from periodic reporting to continuous monitoring has fundamentally changed how organizations operate and make decisions.

The democratization of reporting tools has enabled business users to create their own reports and analyses without requiring technical expertise. Self-service business intelligence platforms allow users to connect to data sources, create visualizations, and share insights with colleagues, like how social media platforms allow anyone to create and share content. This democratization has accelerated the pace of insight generation while reducing the burden on IT departments.

However, the democratization of reporting also introduces new challenges around data governance, quality control, and analytical rigor. When anyone can create reports, organizations must establish processes to ensure that analyses are accurate, consistent, and based on reliable data sources. It's like the challenge social media platforms face in ensuring that user-generated content is accurate and trustworthy.

2.5.2 The Art and Science of Data Visualization

Data visualization transforms abstract numbers into visual patterns that human brains can quickly process and understand. However, effective visualization requires more than simply creating charts, demands understanding of human perception, cognitive psychology, and communication principles.

Think about the difference between reading a paragraph describing the weather forecast and looking at a weather map with colors showing temperature and symbols showing precipitation. Visual representation allows you to quickly understand complex information that would take much longer to process in text form. The same principle applies to business data—effective visualizations can communicate complex patterns and relationships much more efficiently than tables of numbers.

The choice of visualization type significantly impacts the message communicated by data. Bar charts excel at comparing quantities across categories, like comparing sales performance across different product lines. Line charts effectively show trends over time, like tracking customer satisfaction scores over several months. Scatter plots reveal relationships between variables, like showing the relationship between advertising spending and sales results. Heat maps highlight patterns in large datasets, like showing which products sell best in which geographic regions.

Using inappropriate chart types can obscure important patterns or mislead viewers about the data's meaning. For example, using a pie chart to show trends over time would be confusing because pie charts are designed to show parts of a whole, not changes over time. Similarly, using a line chart to compare unrelated categories would be misleading because line charts imply a continuous relationship between data points.

Color usage in data visualization requires particular attention to both aesthetic and functional considerations. Colors should enhance understanding rather than merely decorating charts. Effective color schemes use contrast to highlight important information, maintain consistency across related visualizations, and remain accessible to viewers with color vision deficiencies.

Context plays a crucial role in effective data visualization. Numbers without context are difficult to interpret—a 10% increase in sales might be excellent performance during a recession but disappointing during an economic boom. Effective visualizations provide appropriate context through comparison to targets, historical performance, or industry benchmarks.

2.5.3 Interactive and Dynamic Visualizations

Static visualizations provide valuable insights but limit users to the specific view chosen by the creator. Interactive visualizations enable users to explore data from multiple perspectives, drilling down into details or filtering to focus on specific segments of interest.

Drill-down capabilities allow users to move from summary views to detailed analysis. A sales dashboard might show overall revenue performance at the top level, with the ability to drill down to regional performance, then individual store performance, then specific product performance. This progressive disclosure approach accommodates different user needs and analytical depths, similar to how a GPS navigation system can show you a broad view of your route or zoom in to show detailed street-level information.

Filtering and segmentation capabilities enable users to focus on specific subsets of data. A customer analytics dashboard might allow filtering by customer segment, geographic region, or time period. These capabilities transform single visualizations into multiple analytical views, like having adjustable filters on a camera that allow you to see the same scene in different ways.

Real-time data integration creates dynamic visualizations that update automatically as new data becomes available. Manufacturing dashboards might show current production rates, quality metrics, and equipment status that update every few minutes. This real-time capability enables immediate response to operational issues, similar to how traffic apps update in real-time to help you avoid congestion.

2.5.4 How AI is Changing Business Analytics

Artificial intelligence is revolutionizing descriptive analytics by automating many tasks that previously required human analysts. AI-powered tools can automatically identify significant patterns in data, generate written summaries of key findings, and even suggest areas for further investigation.

Natural language generation technology can automatically create written summaries of data patterns, transforming charts and tables into readable narratives. These automated summaries can highlight key trends, identify significant changes, and explain the business implications of data patterns. For example, an AI system might generate a summary stating: "Sales revenue increased 12% compared to last month, driven primarily by strong performance in the Northeast region where new product launches exceeded expectations by 25%."

This capability is like having a smart assistant that can look at complex data and explain it to you in plain English. Instead of spending time trying to interpret charts and tables, managers can read automatically generated summaries that highlight the most important insights and their business implications.

Automated anomaly detection algorithms can continuously monitor business metrics and alert managers when unusual patterns occur. These systems learn normal patterns in data and flag deviations that might indicate problems or opportunities. A retail company might use anomaly detection to identify stores with unusual sales patterns that warrant investigation, like how credit card companies use automated systems to detect potentially fraudulent transactions.

Pattern recognition capabilities enable AI systems to identify complex relationships in data that might not be apparent to human analysts. Machine learning algorithms can analyze thousands of variables simultaneously to identify factors that correlate with business outcomes. These insights can guide further investigation and hypothesis development.

However, AI-assisted analytics also introduces new challenges around interpretability and trust. Black-box algorithms that provide insights without explanation can be difficult to validate and may not be acceptable in situations where understanding the reasoning behind decisions is important. The field of explainable AI focuses on developing techniques that provide both accurate insights and understandable explanations.

2.5.5 Building Automated Reporting Systems

Automated reporting systems can generate and distribute reports on predetermined schedules, ensuring that stakeholders receive timely information without manual intervention. These systems can customize report content based on recipient roles and preferences, delivering relevant information to each user.

Exception reporting focuses on identifying and highlighting unusual patterns or performance deviations. Rather than overwhelming users with comprehensive data, exception reports draw attention to areas that require investigation or action. A financial controller might receive automated alerts when expenses exceed budget thresholds or when key ratios fall outside acceptable ranges.

Threshold-based alerting systems monitor key metrics continuously and send notifications when predefined conditions are met. These systems enable proactive management by identifying issues before they become serious problems. A customer service manager might receive alerts when call wait times exceed targets or when customer satisfaction scores drop below acceptable levels.

The integration of multiple communication channels enables automated systems to deliver information through the most appropriate medium for each situation. Routine reports might be delivered via email, urgent alerts might be sent via text message, and detailed analyses might be posted to collaboration platforms.

2.5.6 The Importance of Data-Driven Culture

Successful implementation of modern reporting and visualization capabilities requires more than just technology—it demands cultural change and organizational commitment to data-driven decision-making. This transformation involves training, change management, and ongoing support for users at all levels.

Data literacy training helps employees understand how to interpret and act on analytical insights. This training should cover basic statistical concepts, visualization interpretation, and critical thinking about data quality and limitations. However, data literacy training must be tailored to different roles and responsibilities within the organization.

The concept of analytical storytelling emphasizes the importance of communication skills in addition to technical capabilities. The most sophisticated analyses are worthless if they cannot be communicated effectively to decision-makers. Organizations must invest in developing both analytical and communication skills among their teams.

Success metrics for reporting initiatives should focus on business outcomes rather than just technical capabilities. Rather than measuring the number of reports created or dashboards deployed, organizations should assess whether reporting capabilities are improving decision-making and business performance.

2.6 Conclusion

Descriptive analytics provides the essential foundation for understanding business performance. By recognizing key performance indicators, interpreting dashboards, and identifying trends, patterns, and variances, organizations can transform raw data into actionable insights. This module has shown how these skills allow businesses to track progress, uncover opportunities for improvement, and communicate results effectively. Modern tools, including AI-powered analytics, enhance the speed and accessibility of these insights, enabling users to automatically detect patterns, generate summaries, and respond to anomalies in real time. Effective descriptive analytics connects daily operational metrics to strategic objectives, helping employees at all levels understand how their work contributes to overall business success.

Beyond tools and techniques, the true power of descriptive analytics lies in context, interpretation, and communication. Data becomes valuable only when it tells a clear story and informs decision-making. By mastering KPI selection, dashboard design, trend and variance analysis, and visualization, you develop the skills to understand historical performance, assess current outcomes, and lay the groundwork for predictive and prescriptive analytics. As you continue your analytical journey, these competencies will remain critical, empowering you to transform data into insights that drive informed, strategic decisions in any organization.

2.7 Key Terms

Descriptive Analytics – The systematic process of examining historical data to understand what has happened in a business, providing insights into past performance.

Key Performance Indicator (KPI) – A measurable value that indicates how effectively an organization is achieving key business objectives.

Dashboard – A visual interface that presents key metrics and KPIs to enable quick understanding and decision-making.

Trend Analysis – The examination of historical data over time to identify consistent increases, decreases, or patterns.

Seasonal Pattern – Regular and predictable fluctuations in data that repeat over a fixed period, such as holiday sales spikes.

Cyclical Pattern – Data fluctuations occurring over irregular, longer-term periods, often tied to economic or industry cycles.

Variance Analysis – Comparing actual performance to planned or expected performance to identify differences and their causes.

Favorable Variance – When actual performance exceeds expectations or budgeted targets.

Unfavorable Variance – When actual performance falls short of expectations or budgeted targets.

Ratio Analysis – Evaluating relationships between different business metrics to assess efficiency, profitability, or liquidity.

Profitability Ratio – A metric that measures how effectively a company generates profit relative to revenue or costs (e.g., gross profit margin, net profit margin).

Efficiency Ratio – Metrics that assess how well an organization uses its resources (e.g., inventory turnover, accounts receivable turnover).

Liquidity Ratio – Measures a company's ability to meet short-term obligations (e.g., current ratio, quick ratio).

Moving Average – A calculation that averages data over a rolling period to smooth out short-term fluctuations and reveal trends.

Year-over-Year (YoY) Comparison – Comparing a metric for the current period to the same period in the previous year to account for seasonality.

Compound Annual Growth Rate (CAGR) – The mean annual growth rate of a metric over a specified period of time, smoothing out year-to-year fluctuations.

Leading Indicator – A metric that changes before the overall business metric it predicts, allowing proactive decisions.

Lagging Indicator – A metric that changes after the business metric it reflects, confirming trends after they occur.

Data Visualization – The graphical representation of data to reveal patterns, trends, and insights.

Interactive Visualization – Visualizations that allow users to explore data dynamically through filtering, drill-downs, and segmentation.

Artificial Intelligence (AI) – Technology that automates tasks like pattern recognition, anomaly detection, and summarization in data analytics.

Automated Reporting – Systems that generate and distribute reports automatically on predetermined schedules.

Exception Reporting – Highlighting unusual or out-of-range data to focus attention on anomalies or important deviations.

Data-Driven Culture – An organizational mindset where decisions are guided by data analysis rather than intuition alone.

Analytical Storytelling – Communicating insights from data in a clear, compelling way that connects metrics to business outcomes.

2.8 Review Questions

1. What is descriptive analytics, and why is it considered the foundation of all business analytics?
2. Define a Key Performance Indicator (KPI) and give two examples relevant to a retail business.
3. Explain the difference between strategic, tactical, and operational KPIs.
4. What is a business dashboard, and how does it help decision-makers?
5. Describe the difference between seasonal, cyclical, and linear trends in business data.
6. How does variance analysis help organizations understand business performance? Provide an example of a favorable and unfavorable variance.
7. Explain the purpose of ratio analysis and give one example each of profitability, efficiency, and liquidity ratio.
8. What role does data visualization play in descriptive analytics? Give an example of a chart type and the kind of data it is best suited for.
9. How are AI tools transforming descriptive analytics? Provide two examples of AI applications in this context.
10. Why is building a data-driven culture important for modern organizations, and how does analytical storytelling support it?

2.9 References

[1] Matellio. (2024). *Essential List of Data Analytics Tools for 2024.* https://www.matellio.com/blog/list-of-data-analytics-tools/

[2] Emeritus. (2024). *6 Emerging Business Analytics Trends to Watch for in 2024.* https://emeritus.org/in/learn/business-analytics-trends/

2.10 Lab 2-1 Descriptive Analytics and KPIs

This lab introduces descriptive analytics through hands-on work with real business data, focusing on how organizations make sense of past performance. You'll explore how raw data becomes meaningful information by calculating key performance indicators (KPIs) and examining patterns across time. Rather than just working through formulas, you'll practice interpreting what the numbers actually say about a business—what's improving, what's declining, and where attention is needed.

As you progress, you'll also learn how to present your findings clearly using simple reports and visualizations, the same tools managers rely on to guide decisions. The lab highlights how dashboards and AI-assisted analysis can streamline this process, helping transform large datasets into concise, actionable insights. By the end, you'll have a stronger understanding of how descriptive analytics supports real-world business decision-making.

2.10.1 Demonstration

This demonstration introduces the process of analyzing a small business dataset using spreadsheet software. The objective is to show how raw numerical information can be transformed into meaningful insights through organization, calculation, and visualization. The dataset represents six months of sales activity, including both actual sales and a consistent monthly target.

The dataset contains three fields: Month, Actual Sales, and Sales Target. The sales target remains constant at 105 units per month, while actual sales vary from January through June. This information will be used to calculate summary statistics, evaluate performance against goals, and create visual representations of trends.

Table 2.6: Monthly sales compared to sales targets

Month	Actual Sales	Sales Target
Jan	95	105
Feb	102	105
Mar	110	105
Apr	108	105
May	115	105
Jun	123	105

2.10.1.1 Step 1: Compute some summary measures

Excel can be used to compute several summary measures. These calculations help interpret the sales data and evaluate performance relative to the monthly target.

2.10.1.1.1 Total Sales

The total sales value represents the sum of all actual sales across the six-month period. To calculate this value in Excel:

1. Select an empty cell below or beside the table.
2. Enter the SUM function referencing the "Actual Sales" column. If the data is formatted as a table, Excel automatically uses the column name in the formula.
3. The formula appears as: =SUM([Actual Sales])

4. Press Enter to display the total.

This result provides a single figure representing overall sales volume for the period.

2.10.1.1.2 Average Monthly Sales

The average monthly sales value indicates the typical sales level per month. It is useful for assessing consistency and identifying whether performance is trending upward or downward.

To calculate the average:

1. Select another empty cell.
2. Enter the AVERAGE function referencing the "Actual Sales" column.
3. The formula appears as: =AVERAGE([Actual Sales])
4. Press Enter to compute the average.

This value summarizes the central tendency of the sales data.

2.10.1.1.3 Sales Variance

Sales variance measures the difference between actual sales and the sales target for each month. Positive values indicate that the target was exceeded, while negative values indicate underperformance.

To calculate variance for each month:

- Insert a new column in the table and label it "Variance."
- In the first row of the new column, enter a formula subtracting the target from the actual sales for that row.
- Press Enter. Because the data is in a table, Excel automatically fills the formula down the entire column.

The completed variance column allows quick comparison of performance across months and highlights where targets were met or exceeded.

Table 2.7: Monthly sales, targets, and variance

Month	Actual Sales	Sales Target	Variance
Jan	95	105	-10
Feb	102	105	-3
Mar	110	105	5
Apr	108	105	3
May	115	105	10
Jun	123	105	18

Month	Actual Sales	Sales Target	Variance
Total	**653**		
Average Monthly Sales	**108.83**		

2.10.1.2 Step 2: Charts and Visual Analysis in Excel

Visualizations play an essential role in interpreting business data. Charts make it easier to identify patterns, compare values, and communicate results. Using the Monthly Sales Performance dataset, two types of charts can be created to highlight different aspects of the information: a line chart to show changes over time and a column chart to illustrate variance from the target.

2.10.1.2.1 Creating a Line Chart: Sales Over Time

A line chart is well suited for displaying how values change across a sequence, such as months in a year. In this dataset, the line chart illustrates the progression of actual sales from January through June.

To create the chart:

1. Select the Month column and the Actual Sales column in the table. These two fields provide the horizontal axis (time) and the vertical axis (sales values).
2. Open the Insert tab on the ribbon.
3. In the Charts group, choose Line Chart and select the basic line chart option.
4. Excel generates a chart showing each month plotted against its corresponding sales value.
5. Add a chart title, such as Sales Over Time, to clarify the purpose of the visualization.

The resulting chart reveals the overall upward trend in sales. It becomes easy to see that sales begin below the target in January and February but rise steadily in the following months. The line chart highlights both the direction and the consistency of the improvement.

2.10.1.2.2 Creating a Column Chart: Variance from Target

A column chart is effective for comparing individual values, especially when evaluating performance against a benchmark. In this case, the benchmark is the monthly sales target of 105 units. The variance column, calculated earlier, provides the data needed for this visualization.

To create the chart:

- Select the Month column and the Variance column in the table.
- Navigate to the Insert tab.
- In the Charts group, choose Column Chart and select a simple clustered column design.
- Excel produces a chart with one column for each month, representing the difference between actual sales and the target.
- Adjust bar fill color so all month labels are visible.
- Add a descriptive title, such as Variance from Target.

In the completed chart, columns extending above zero indicate months in which the target was exceeded, while columns below zero represent months that fell short. This visualization makes it easy to compare performance across months and to identify the point at which the business began consistently surpassing its goal.

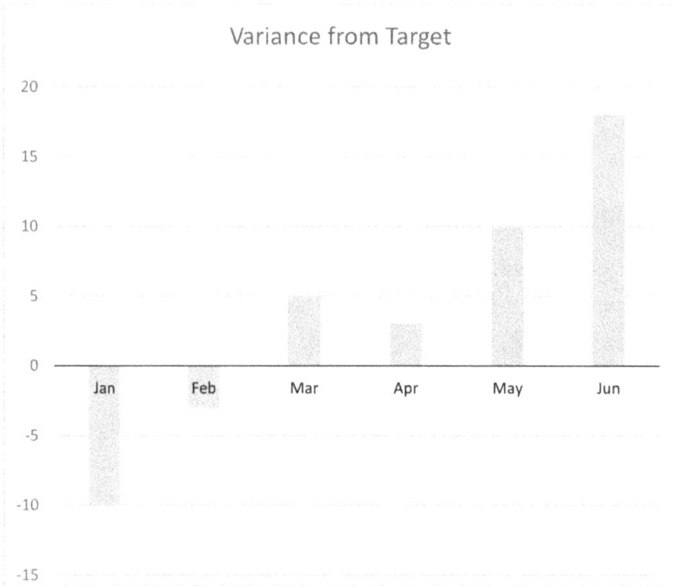

2.10.1.3 Step 3: Interpret results in terms of KPIs

2.10.1.3.1 Key Performance Indicators (KPIs)

Several values in the Monthly Sales Performance dataset function as key performance indicators because they directly measure progress toward the organization's sales objectives.

Total Sales for the Period Across the six-month timeframe, actual sales sum to 653 units. This cumulative figure provides a broad measure of overall output and serves as a reference point for evaluating whether the business is generating sufficient activity to meet its goals.

Average Monthly Sales The average monthly sales value is 108.83 units, calculated by dividing total sales (653) by the six reporting months. This KPI reflects the typical level of monthly performance and helps determine whether sales activity is stable, improving, or declining.

Monthly Variance from Target Variance values indicate how actual sales compare to the monthly target of 105 units. The dataset shows negative variance in January (−10) and February (−3), followed by positive variance in March (5), April (3), May (10), and June (18). These values highlight the transition from early underperformance to consistent target-exceeding results.

Direction and Consistency of the Sales Trend The progression from 95 units in January to 123 units in June demonstrates a clear upward trend. This trend serves as a KPI because it reflects not only month-to-month performance but also the overall trajectory of the business.

2.10.2 Practice

Use the dataset below.

Table 2.8: Monthly actual sales compared to sales targets

Month	Actual Sales	Sales Target
Jan	120	130
Feb	128	130
Mar	135	130
Apr	140	130
May	148	130
Jun	155	130
Jul	160	135
Aug	158	135

2.10.2.1 Questions

1. Using the dataset, calculate the Total Sales for all months. What formula should be used?
2. Calculate the Average Monthly Sales. How does this value help in understanding performance consistency?
3. Add a new column labeled Variance and compute the difference between Actual Sales and Sales Target for each month. What does a positive variance indicate?
4. Identify which months exceeded the sales target and which months fell short.
5. Based on the variance values for each month, determine whether the business is becoming more or less aligned with its sales target over time. Explain which months show the most significant change and what this indicates about overall performance.
6. Create a Line Chart showing Actual Sales over time. What trend does the chart reveal?
7. Create a Column Chart showing Variance from Target. Which months show the highest and lowest variance?
8. Based on your calculations, list the Key Performance Indicators (KPIs) that summarize overall performance.
9. Interpret the results: How do the Total Sales, Average Monthly Sales, and Variance values demonstrate progress toward business goals?
10. Use an AI tool (such as Excel Copilot or another AI assistant) to generate a short summary of the dataset's performance trend. How does the AI's interpretation

compare to your own?

Chapter 3

Diagnostic Analytics

3.1 Learning Outcomes

3-1. Recognize when two things happen together versus when one thing causes another

3-2. Understand how businesses look at data in different ways to find patterns

3-3. Identify basic methods companies use to find the real reasons behind problems

3-4. Recognize how computers help businesses spot unusual patterns and explain what they find

3.2 Introduction

Imagine you work at an online clothing store, and your boss comes to you with some confusing news. Over the past three months, the company has been spending 35% more

money to get new customers to visit the website. At the same time, fewer people who visit the website are buying clothes - the percentage dropped by 18%. The numbers clearly show what happened, but your boss asks you the big question: "Why is this happening?"

This is exactly what diagnostic analytics helps businesses figure out. In Module 2, we learned about descriptive analytics, which tells you what happened in your business. Diagnostic analytics goes one step further - it's like being a detective who investigates why things happened.

Think of it like this: if your phone stops working, descriptive analytics would tell you "your phone is not working." But diagnostic analytics would help you figure out whether the problem is a dead battery, no internet connection, a broken screen, or something else. Without this detective work, you might waste time trying to fix the wrong thing.

Going back to our clothing store example, the investigation might show that the company started advertising on newer social media platforms around the same time costs went up. But just because these two things happened at the same time doesn't mean one caused the other. Maybe the real problem was that the company changed who they were trying to reach as customers, and these new customers don't actually shop on those social media platforms. Meanwhile, fewer people buying things might be because the website was having technical problems during the same time period.

This kind of detective work is really important because without it, companies often try to fix the wrong things. This wastes money and means the problems keep happening. Studies show that companies that are good at figuring out why things happen are much more likely to reach their business goals.

The tools that help businesses do this detective work have gotten much better with advances in computer technology and artificial intelligence. Modern tools can automatically spot unusual patterns and even suggest possible explanations for what's happening in the data. However, these new technologies also bring challenges around understanding what the results mean and making sure we can trust what they tell us.

In this chapter, we'll explore how businesses investigate problems using data. We'll learn the difference between things that just happen to occur at the same time versus things that cause each other. We'll see how companies look at their data from different angles to find hidden patterns. We'll understand the basic methods businesses use to find the real reasons behind their problems. And we'll recognize how computer systems help speed up these investigations.

Whether you're looking at why sales are going down, trying to understand customer behavior, or investigating any other business problem, these concepts will help you understand how businesses turn confusing data into clear answers. The ability to answer "why" questions is what separates people who can read basic reports from people who can help solve business problems.

3.3 Correlation and Causation

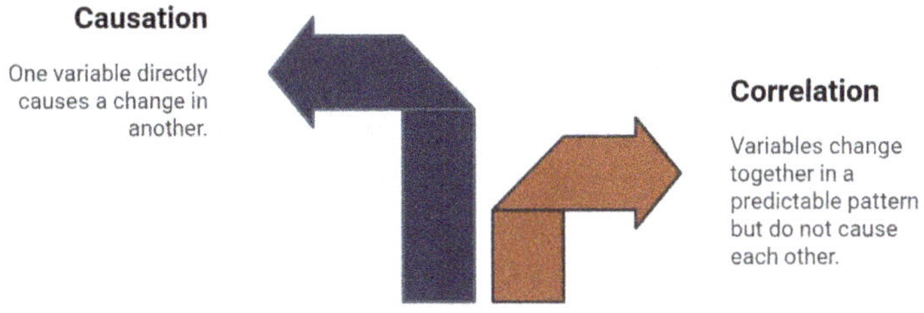

3.3.1 Why This Difference Matters

One of the most important ideas in business analytics is understanding the difference between correlation and causation. This might sound complicated, but it's something you encounter in everyday life. Getting this wrong can lead to expensive business mistakes.

Correlation means that two things tend to happen together or change together in a predictable way. For example, when it gets hot outside, both ice cream sales and the number of people going swimming tend to increase. These two things are correlated - they happen together.

Causation means that one thing directly causes another thing to happen. For example, when you turn on a light switch, it causes the light to turn on. The switch directly makes the light work.

Here's where it gets tricky: just because two things happen together doesn't mean one causes the other. Going back to our ice cream and swimming example - ice cream sales and swimming both increase when it's hot, but eating ice cream doesn't cause people to go swimming. Both are caused by a third thing: hot weather.

This same type of thinking applies to business all the time. Let's say a coffee shop notices that on days when they sell more coffee, they also get more customer complaints. The coffee sales and complaints are correlated - they happen together. But does selling more coffee cause more complaints? Not necessarily. Maybe both happen on busy days when the staff is rushed and makes more mistakes.

Understanding this difference is crucial for businesses because it affects what they should do to solve problems. If the coffee shop thinks that selling more coffee causes complaints, they might try to sell less coffee. But if the real problem is being understaffed on busy days, they should hire more employees instead.

3.3.2 Real Examples from Business

Let's look at some real examples of correlation versus causation that businesses encounter:

A technology company might notice that employees who work longer hours get better performance reviews. The correlation is clear - longer hours and better reviews happen together. But does working longer hours cause better performance? Maybe, but there could be other explanations. Perhaps the employees who work longer hours are more motivated, have more experience, or work on more important projects.

A retail store might observe that customers who spend more time in the store tend to buy more items. Time in store and purchases are correlated. But does spending more time cause people to buy more? It's possible, but maybe customers who are already planning to buy a lot of things naturally spend more time looking around.

An online company might find that customers who use their mobile app spend more money than customers who only use the website. App usage and spending are correlated. But does using the app cause people to spend more? Maybe the app is just more convenient for people who were already big spenders.

3.3.3 How Businesses Test for Real Cause-and-Effect

The best way for businesses to figure out if one thing really causes another is through experiments. Think of this like the science experiments you might have done in school, where you change one thing and see what happens to something else.

A/B testing is the most common type of business experiment. Here's how it works: a company randomly shows different versions of something (like a website design) to different groups of customers. Then they measure what happens. Because customers are randomly assigned to each group, any differences in behavior can be attributed to the different versions.

For example, an online store might randomly show half their visitors a red ”Buy Now” button and half their visitors a blue ”Buy Now” button. If more people click the red button, they can be confident that the color caused the difference.

However, businesses can't always do experiments. Sometimes it would be unethical (like deliberately providing bad customer service to see what happens). Sometimes it's just not practical (like testing whether a major company reorganization improves performance).

When businesses can't do experiments, they look for ”natural experiments” - situations where something changed for reasons outside the company's control. For example, if a new law affects some states but not others, a company can compare what happened in different states to understand the law's impact.

3.3.4 Simple Ways to Think About Cause-and-Effect

There are some basic questions businesses ask to figure out if one thing might cause another:

Timing: Did the cause happen before the effect? If a marketing campaign is supposed to increase sales, the campaign should start before sales go up. This seems obvious, but sometimes the effects of business actions take time to show up.

Strength: How strong is the relationship? If two things are very strongly connected, it's more likely that one causes the other. But even weak relationships can sometimes be causal.

Consistency: Does the same relationship show up in different situations? If a pricing strategy works in multiple stores and different time periods, it's more likely to be truly effective.

Logic: Does the proposed cause-and-effect relationship make sense? If someone claims that playing music in a store causes people to buy more expensive items, we can think about whether this makes logical sense based on what we know about human behavior.

Understanding these basic principles helps you think more critically about business claims and data. When someone says, "A causes B," you can ask yourself: Did A happen before B? How strong is the relationship? Does it happen consistently? Does it make logical sense?

3.4 Looking at Data from Different Angles

3.4.1 Breaking Down Big Numbers into Smaller Pieces

When businesses look at their overall performance, they often see big summary numbers that don't tell the whole story. Drill-down analysis is like using a magnifying glass to look at these big numbers more closely. It helps businesses figure out which specific parts of their business are driving the overall results.

Think of it like getting a report card that shows your overall grade average. If your average dropped, you'd want to know which subjects caused the problem. Maybe your math grade went down while your other grades stayed the same. Then you might look even closer to see which specific math tests or assignments caused the problem. Each level of detail gives you different information about what you need to fix.

Businesses do the same thing with their data. A company might see that overall customer satisfaction dropped by 5%. But when they look more closely, they might discover that satisfaction actually improved for most customers, while dropping dramatically for one specific group. This tells them exactly where to focus their improvement efforts.

The key is understanding that business data is organized like a pyramid. At the top, you have big summary numbers. As you go down the pyramid, you get more and more detailed information. A restaurant chain might start by looking at total sales across all locations, then look at sales by region, then by individual restaurants, then by different menu items.

The way you choose to break down the data makes a big difference in what you discover. The same sales data could be analyzed by location, by time period, by customer type, or by product category. Each way of looking at it might reveal different patterns and suggest different explanations.

3.4.2 Understanding Different Types of Customers

One of the most powerful ways businesses break down their data is by looking at different groups of customers. This is called customer segmentation, and it helps companies understand that not all customers are the same.

There are several common ways businesses group their customers:

Demographics means grouping customers by characteristics like age, income, or where they live. A clothing store might find that younger customers prefer different styles than older customers, or that customers in different cities have different preferences.

Behavior means grouping customers by what they actually do. This might include how often they buy things, how much they spend, or how they use products. An online streaming service might group customers by how many hours they watch per week or what types of shows they prefer.

Value means grouping customers by how much they're worth to the business. Some customers might buy a lot and rarely return items, while others might buy less frequently but spend more money each time.

Understanding these different customer groups helps businesses make better decisions. Instead of treating all customers the same way, they can customize their approach for different groups.

3.4.3 A Real Example: Investigating Customer Satisfaction

Let's look at how a telecommunications company (like Verizon or AT&T) might investigate why their customer satisfaction scores are dropping. This example shows how breaking down data reveals insights that wouldn't be visible in the overall numbers.

Step 1: Looking at Different Customer Types

The company first looks at satisfaction scores for business customers versus residential customers:

Customer Type	Satisfaction Score
Business	7.65
Residential	7.39

This shows that residential customers are less satisfied than business customers. This gives the company a clue about where to focus their investigation.

Step 2: Looking at Different Service Types

Next, they break down the data by the type of service customers have:

Customer Type	Service Type	Satisfaction Score
Business	Bundled Services	7.81
Business	Single Service	7.42
Residential	Bundled Services	7.05
Residential	Single Service	7.73

This reveals something interesting: business customers are more satisfied when they have bundled services (multiple services like internet, TV, and phone together), but residential customers are less satisfied with bundled services. This suggests the company might have different problems with how they deliver bundled services to residential customers.

Step 3: Looking at Different Geographic Areas

The company then looks at satisfaction by geographic region:

Customer Type	Service Type	Region	Satisfaction Score
Residential	Bundled Services	Rural	7.42
Residential	Bundled Services	Suburban	7.34
Residential	Bundled Services	Urban	6.33

Now they can see that the problem is concentrated in urban areas. Residential customers with bundled services in cities are much less satisfied (6.33) than the same type of customers in rural areas (7.42).

Step 4: Looking at When the Problem Started

Finally, they look at how satisfaction changed over time:

Month	Satisfaction Score
1	7.61
2	7.44
3	7.90
4	7.58
5	7.61
6	7.67
7	7.39
8	7.19
9	7.11
10	7.43
11	7.35
12	7.23

The data shows that satisfaction was highest in months 3 and 6, then started declining consistently from month 7 onward. The company remembers that they did a major system upgrade between months 6 and 7.

3.4.4 What This Investigation Revealed

By breaking down their data in different ways, the telecommunications company discovered that their satisfaction problem wasn't affecting all customers equally. The problem was concentrated among residential customers with bundled services in urban areas, and it started right after a system upgrade.

This targeted insight helps the company focus their improvement efforts. Instead of trying to fix everything for everyone, they can concentrate on urban network capacity, bundled service integration, and residential customer support - the specific areas where the problems are occurring.

This example shows the power of looking at data from different angles. The overall satisfaction decline of 0.6 points didn't tell the whole story. Only by breaking down the data could the company identify exactly where the problems were occurring and when they started.

3.5 Finding the Real Reasons Behind Problems

3.5.1 A Systematic Way to Investigate Problems

When businesses have problems, they need a systematic way to find the real causes rather than just treating the symptoms. Root cause analysis is like being a detective - you gather clues, ask questions, and keep digging until you find the real source of the problem.

Think about when you get sick. Taking medicine for a headache might make you feel better temporarily, but if the headache is caused by not drinking enough water, the headache will keep coming back until you address the real cause - dehydration. Businesses face the same challenge. They need to find and fix the underlying causes of problems, not just the obvious symptoms.

The first step in any good investigation is clearly defining what the problem is. This means being specific about what happened, when it happened, where it happened, and what the impact was. Without a clear problem definition, investigations can go in circles and waste time.

One of the simplest but most powerful investigation techniques is called the ”5 Whys.” You start with the problem and keep asking ”why” until you get to the root cause. Here's how a manufacturing company might use this technique to investigate increased product defects:

- Why are defect rates increasing? Because quality control is catching more problems.
- Why is quality control catching more problems? Because we improved our inspection process.
- Why did we improve our inspection process? Because customers were complaining about quality.

- Why were customers complaining about quality? Because we started using a new supplier for key parts.
- Why did we start using a new supplier? Because our old supplier couldn't keep up with increased demand.

This investigation reveals that the apparent increase in defects might actually be good news - they're just detecting problems that were already there. The real issue is supplier management and capacity planning.

3.5.2 Visual Tools for Problem Investigation

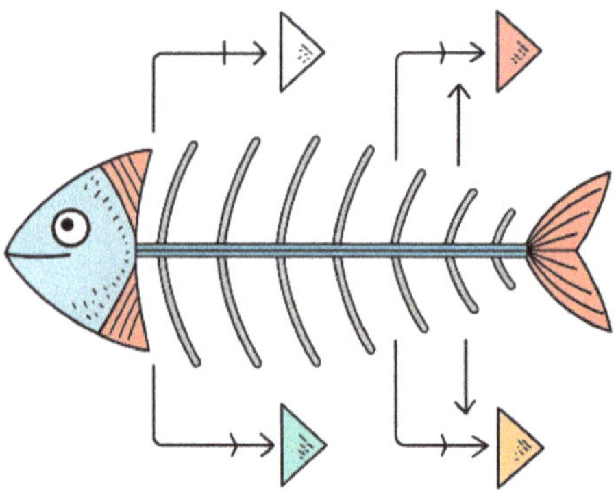

Sometimes it helps to draw out all the possible causes of a problem. A fishbone diagram (also called an Ishikawa diagram) is a visual tool that looks like a fish skeleton. The problem goes at the "head" of the fish, and all the possible causes branch off like "bones."

The traditional categories for organizing causes are:

- **People**: Issues related to training, skills, or motivation
- **Process**: Problems with procedures or workflows
- **Materials**: Issues with supplies or components
- **Equipment**: Problems with tools or machinery
- **Environment**: Issues with the physical or business environment
- **Methods**: Problems with how work gets done

For example, if a software company's mobile app is losing users, they might organize potential causes like this:

People factors: Users don't know how to use new features, changing user preferences, or different types of people using the app.

Process factors: Complicated sign-up process, confusing navigation, or poor customer support.

Technology factors: App crashes, slow performance, or compatibility problems with new phones.

Environment factors: New competitors, changes in the market, or new regulations.

This visual approach helps ensure that investigators consider all possible causes, not just the obvious ones.

3.5.3 Using Data to Guide Investigations

Modern businesses increasingly use data analysis to guide their problem investigations. While you don't need to understand the technical details, it's helpful to know what these techniques can reveal.

Correlation analysis identifies which factors tend to change together with the problem. If customer complaints increase at the same time as response times, this suggests a relationship worth investigating further.

Time analysis looks at how problems develop over time and can help identify when changes occurred that might have triggered the issue. If problems started right after a new policy was implemented, that policy becomes a prime suspect.

Pattern detection uses computer algorithms to automatically identify unusual patterns that might provide clues about causes. These systems can spot relationships that humans might miss.

3.5.4 An Example of Real Investigation

Let's look at how a customer service organization investigated declining satisfaction scores. This example shows how multiple investigation techniques work together.

The Problem: Customer satisfaction scores dropped from 8.2 to 7.6 over three months.

Initial Data Analysis: The team looked at correlations between different factors:

Month	Satisfaction Score
1	7.61
2	7.44
3	7.90
4	7.58
5	7.61
6	7.67
7	7.39
8	7.19
9	7.11

Month	Satisfaction Score
10	7.43
11	7.35
12	7.23

The weak correlations suggested that response time and issue complexity weren't the main drivers of the satisfaction decline.

Sample Investigation: Looking at individual customer service tickets revealed significant variation:

Ticket	Product	Agent	Response Time (min)	Satisfaction	Issue Complexity
1	C	Agent 10	33.8	6.8	2
2	C	Agent 6	15.4	8.5	5
3	C	Agent 10	22.9	9.2	3

The data showed that Agent 10 had consistently longer response times, and satisfaction varied significantly across different products and agents.

Key Findings: The investigation revealed:

- **Agent Performance Variation**: Some agents consistently performed better than others
- **Product-Specific Issues**: Customers with Product C were more sensitive to response time delays
- **Training Gaps**: Inconsistent performance suggested training problems

Recommended Actions: Based on these findings, the company decided to:

- Provide additional training for underperforming agents
- Develop specialized procedures for Product C support
- Review of how cases are assigned to agents
- Create better performance monitoring

This investigation shows how combining different analytical approaches reveals insights that might be missed by looking at any single factor alone.

3.6 How Computers Help Investigate Business Problems

3.6.1 The Rise of Smart Computer Systems

Artificial intelligence and machine learning have changed how businesses investigate problems. These computer systems can look at huge amounts of data much faster than humans and spot patterns that people might miss. Think of them as super-powered assistants that never get tired and can examine thousands of pieces of information at once.

While a human analyst might take days to look through customer service data searching for patterns, an AI system can do the same work in minutes. These systems are particularly good at finding complex relationships between different factors that might not be obvious to human investigators.

However, these smart systems also have limitations. They need high-quality data to work properly, and they can sometimes find patterns that don't actually mean anything. They also can't always explain their findings in ways that humans can easily understand. This is why businesses still need people to interpret and act on what the computers discover.

The key advantage of AI systems is that they can continuously monitor business data and automatically alert managers when something unusual happens. Instead of waiting for monthly reports, businesses can know about problems as soon as they start developing.

3.6.2 Automatic Problem Detection

One of the most useful applications of AI in business investigation is anomaly detection - automatically spotting when something unusual is happening. These systems learn what "normal" looks like for a business and then flag anything that deviates significantly from normal patterns.

For example, a retail company might use anomaly detection to automatically identify stores with unusual sales patterns. If one store's sales suddenly drop by 30% while other similar stores remain stable, the system would flag this for investigation. The unusual pattern might indicate problems with staffing, inventory, local competition, or equipment.

These systems can monitor many different aspects of business performance simultaneously:

- Sales patterns that deviate from seasonal norms
- Customer behavior that differs from typical patterns
- Operational metrics that fall outside normal ranges
- Financial indicators that show unexpected changes

The advantage of automated detection is speed. Instead of discovering problems weeks later in monthly reports, businesses can identify and address issues within hours or days of when they start occurring.

3.6.3 AI That Explains What It Finds

One challenge with AI systems is that they sometimes work like "black boxes" - they can identify patterns but can't always explain why those patterns are important. This has led to the development of "explainable AI" - systems that can provide understandable explanations for their findings.

For example, an AI system analyzing customer cancellations might generate an explanation like: "Customer cancellations increased 15% this month. The main factors were customers who had technical support problems in the past 30 days. Customers with more than 2 support tickets and response times longer than 24 hours were most likely to cancel."

This type of explanation helps business managers understand not just what the AI system found, but why it's important and what they might do about it.

Natural language generation allows AI systems to automatically write reports in plain English. Instead of presenting complex charts and statistics, these systems can create summaries that non-technical managers can easily understand.

3.6.4 Pattern Recognition Capabilities

AI systems are highly effective at identifying complex patterns in large datasets, which helps businesses investigate problems faster and uncover insights that might otherwise go unnoticed. Clustering algorithms, for example, can automatically group similar customers, products, or situations based on multiple characteristics. This allows organizations to spot patterns, such as groups of customers with similar complaints, and address the underlying issues affecting those segments.

Association analysis and sequential pattern analysis further enhance investigations. Association analysis can reveal relationships between events—for instance, customers who buy certain product combinations may be more likely to return items. Sequential pattern analysis identifies recurring sequences of events, such as website errors that lead to abandoned shopping carts, helping businesses understand potential cause-and-effect relationships.

Text analysis extends these capabilities to unstructured data sources, including customer reviews, support tickets, and social media comments. By processing large volumes of text, businesses can detect common themes, trends, and sentiment patterns, providing a deeper understanding of customer behavior and operational challenges. Together, these AI techniques enable faster, more accurate, and actionable insights than traditional analysis alone.

3.6.5 Implementing AI Investigation Tools

Successfully using AI for business investigation requires more than just software; organizations need high-quality data, validation processes, and skilled people to interpret results. AI handles large data processing and pattern detection, but humans provide context, validate findings, and act. Ongoing monitoring ensures models remain accurate, and training helps employees understand and trust AI outputs.

3.6.6 The Future of AI in Business Investigation

AI capabilities continue to evolve rapidly. Natural language processing is making it easier for non-technical users to ask questions of data systems using plain English. Computer vision is enabling analysis of visual data like images and videos.

Cloud-based AI services are making sophisticated analytics accessible to smaller businesses that previously couldn't afford such capabilities. Companies can now access powerful analytical tools without major upfront investments in technology or specialized staff.

However, successful AI adoption requires organizational commitment beyond just technology. Companies must develop processes for working effectively with AI systems and address important considerations around data privacy and ethical use of AI insights.

The most successful applications combine human judgment with AI capabilities. AI systems excel at processing data and identifying patterns, while humans provide context, strategic thinking, and decision-making. This partnership approach creates more effective investigative capabilities than either humans or AI could achieve alone.

3.7 Conclusion

In this module, we learned that understanding the difference between correlation and causation is critical for making informed business decisions. Simply observing that two events occur together is not enough to conclude that one causes the other. Businesses that can accurately identify real cause-and-effect relationships avoid wasting resources on ineffective solutions. Using techniques like A/B testing, natural experiments, and systematic root cause analysis, companies can uncover the true drivers behind problems and take targeted actions. Diagnostic analytics, drill-down analysis, and customer segmentation are all essential tools in breaking down complex data into actionable insights.

Modern technologies, including AI and machine learning, have greatly enhanced businesses' ability to detect patterns, identify anomalies, and explain findings quickly. While AI can process vast datasets and highlight relationships humans might miss, human interpretation remains crucial for ensuring insights are meaningful and actionable. The combination of human judgment and computational power allows organizations to investigate problems effectively, make data-driven decisions, and continuously improve business performance. By applying these principles, analysts can move beyond merely reporting numbers to understanding the ”why” behind business outcomes.

3.8 Key Terms

Correlation – A relationship where two variables change together, without necessarily one causing the other.

Causation – A relationship where one event directly causes another.

Diagnostic Analytics – Analysis that investigates the reasons behind observed business outcomes.

Drill-Down Analysis – Breaking aggregate data into smaller parts to find detailed insights.

Customer Segmentation – Grouping customers based on demographics, behavior, or value.

Root Cause Analysis – Systematic process to identify the true cause of a problem.

5 Whys Technique – Asking “why” repeatedly to uncover the underlying cause.

Fishbone Diagram – A visual tool for mapping possible causes of a problem.

A/B Testing – Experiment comparing two versions of a product or process to see which performs better.

Anomaly Detection – Using AI or statistical methods to spot unusual patterns in data.

3.9 Review Questions

1. What is the difference between correlation and causation?
2. Why is it risky for businesses to assume correlation implies causation?
3. How does diagnostic analytics go beyond descriptive analytics?
4. What is drill-down analysis, and how does it help in problem-solving?
5. How can customer segmentation reveal insights that overall data averages cannot?
6. Explain how the “5 Whys” technique works in root cause analysis.
7. What role does a fishbone diagram play in investigating business problems?
8. How can A/B testing help determine causal relationships in business decisions?
9. What are some limitations of AI in business investigations?
10. Why is human interpretation still essential when using AI tools for pattern detection?

3.10 References

[1] Sprinkle Data. (2024). *Diagnostic Analytics: Unlocking Deeper Insights for Informed Decision-Making.* https://www.sprinkledata.com/blogs/diagnostic-analytics-unlocking-deeper-insights-for-informed-decision-making

[2] Data Hub Analytics. (2024). *The Rise of Explainable AI (XAI) in Data Analytics.* https://datahubanalytics.com/the-rise-of-explainable-ai-xai-in-data-analytics/

[3] Management Consulted. (2024). *Correlation vs Causation: Why It Matters For Businesses.* https://managementconsulted.com/correlation-vs-causation/

[4] Sara's Analytics. (2024). *A Step-by-Step Guide to Customer Segmentation Analysis.* https://www.sarasanalytics.com/blog/customer-segmentation-analysis

[5] RTS Labs. (2024). *AI Anomaly Detection: Benefits, Types, Use Cases and Implementation.* https://rtslabs.com/ai-anomaly-detection/

[6] Prosci. (2024). *The Power of Root Cause Analysis and Change Management.* https://www.prosci.com/blog/root-cause-analysis

3.11 Lab 3-1 Diagnostic Analytics Basics

In this lab, you will practice the core skills of diagnostic analytics by investigating why an online clothing retailer’s performance has weakened over time. While descriptive analytics shows what happened, diagnostic analytics focuses on uncovering why it happened by examining patterns, comparing groups, and ruling out incorrect explanations.

You will begin by calculating revenue for each row of activity, then build PivotTables and charts to summarize performance across months. From there, you will compare trends in traffic and revenue, measure correlations between key variables, and break the data down by marketing channel and region to reveal patterns hidden in the overall averages. By the end of the lab, you will be able to identify where performance is declining, which segments are driving the problem, and why higher traffic did not lead to stronger financial results.

3.11.1 Demonstration

Table 3.7: Marketing channel performance metrics by region

Month	Marketing Channel	Region	Website Visitors	Conversion Rate	Average Order Value
1	Search Ads	Urban	1800	0.045	72
1	Social Media	Urban	2100	0.032	68
1	Email	Urban	950	0.058	81
...	...	...	...	...	...

3.11.1.1 Step 1: Compute revenue

To begin the analysis, add a new column to the dataset called Revenue. This column calculates how much money each row of activity generated. Revenue is based on three existing fields: the number of website visitors, the conversion rate, and the average order value. The conversion rate shows what fraction of visitors made a purchase, and the average order value shows how much each purchaser spent. In Excel, click into the first empty cell in the Revenue column and enter the formula that multiplies these three values together. For example, if Website Visitors is in column D, Conversion Rate is in column E, and Average Order Value is in column F, the formula will be for the first data row (row 2 of sheet):

= D2 * E2 * F2

The result will be 5832. Press Enter, then copy the formula down the entire column so that every row calculates its own revenue.

3.11.1.2 Step 2: Create an Overall Performance Summary

Next, create a PivotTable to summarize the dataset and compare performance across months. Select the entire table of data, then insert a PivotTable on a new worksheet. In the PivotTable Fields pane, drag Month into the Rows area so each month appears as its own line. Then add Website Visitors to the Values area and ensure it is summarized as a Sum, since you want the total number of visitors for each month. Add Revenue to the

Values area as well, also summarized as a Sum, so you can compare total revenue across months. Finally, add Conversion Rate to the Values area and change its calculation to Average, which shows the typical conversion rate for each month rather than adding the percentages together.

Table 3.8: Summary of website traffic and performance by category

Category	Total Website Visitors	Total Revenue	Average Conversion Rate
1	11810	39884.16	0.04856
6	12930	41172.52	0.04611
12	14920	39669.70	0.04100
Grand Total	**39660**	**120726.38**	**0.04522**

Month 12 shows the highest number of website visitors (14,920) but does not produce the highest revenue. Revenue actually peaks in Month 6, even though Month 6 has fewer visitors. This indicates that higher traffic did not translate into higher financial performance. The decline in revenue relative to traffic suggests that conversion rate or customer spending weakened in Month 12, and additional analysis is needed to determine why.

3.11.1.3 Step 3: Visualize Trends

To examine how performance changes across the year, begin by copying the monthly summary from your PivotTable into a normal worksheet range. Select the Month, Revenue, and Website Visitors values from the PivotTable, then paste them as Values in a blank area and edit months to have 'M' (change 1 to M1, etc). This step is important because charts created directly from a PivotTable become PivotCharts, which force all metrics onto a single axis and make the trends difficult to interpret.

Once the values are pasted, create two separate line charts. First, highlight the Month and Revenue columns from the pasted range and insert a standard line chart to show how total revenue changes across the three months. Then highlight the Month and Website Visitors columns and insert a second line chart to display how traffic levels change over the same period.

After both charts are created, compare their shapes. Look for months where the two lines move in the same direction and months where they diverge. Divergence is especially important: if website visitors increase but revenue declines, it indicates that higher traffic did not lead to stronger financial performance, suggesting that factors such as conversion rate or customer spending may have changed.

When the two line charts are compared, the key insight is that website visitors increase steadily from Month 1 to Month 12, while revenue does not follow the same upward pattern. In particular, traffic rises sharply between Month 6 and Month 12, yet revenue declines over that same interval. This divergence shows that higher traffic did not translate into stronger financial performance, indicating that another factor—such as a drop in conversion rate or a change in customer spending—must have shifted during this period. The charts demonstrate that traffic alone cannot explain revenue outcomes, and meaningful analysis requires examining additional metrics to understand why performance weakened despite increased visitor volume.

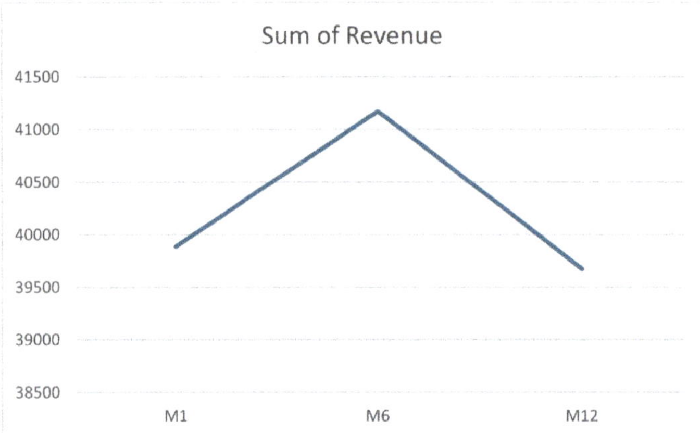

3.11.1.4 Step 4: Demonstrate Correlation

Use Excel's CORREL function to measure how strongly two variables move together. First, calculate the correlation between Website Visitors and Revenue to see whether months with higher traffic tend to generate higher revenue. Then calculate the correlation between Conversion Rate and Revenue to examine whether changes in conversion rate are more closely aligned with revenue performance.

Table 3.9: Correlation between key website performance metrics

Variable 1	Variable 2	Correlation (R)
Website Visitors	Revenue	0.34718
Conversion Rate	Revenue	-0.08675

The correlation between Website Visitors and Revenue is 0.347, which represents a weak positive relationship. This means that months with higher traffic tend to have slightly higher revenue, but the relationship is not strong or consistent. Traffic alone does not reliably predict revenue in this dataset.

The correlation between Conversion Rate and Revenue is -0.087, which is very close to zero. This indicates no meaningful linear relationship between conversion rate and revenue across the three months. In other words, changes in conversion rate do not consistently move with changes in revenue in this small sample.

These results illustrate an important analytical principle: correlation describes patterns, not causes. A strong correlation (values close to 1 or -1) indicates that two variables move together consistently, while a weak correlation (values near 0) shows little or no predictable relationship. Even when correlation is strong, it does not prove that one variable causes the other. Correlation helps narrow possible explanations, but additional analysis is required before drawing conclusions about why revenue changed.

3.11.1.5 Step 5: Drill Down by Channel and Region

To uncover patterns that are hidden in the overall averages, create two sets of PivotTables that break the data into smaller, more meaningful groups.

3.11.1.5.1 A. Summarize Performance by Marketing Channel

1. Select the full dataset, including the Revenue column you added.
2. Insert a PivotTable on a new worksheet.
3. Place Marketing Channel in the Rows area.
4. Add Revenue to the Values area and set it to Sum.
5. Add Conversion Rate to the Values area and set it to Average.

Table 3.10: Revenue and conversion rate by marketing channel

Marketing Channel	Total Revenue	Average Conversion Rate
Email	37483.68	0.05922
Search Ads	46866.52	0.04456

Marketing Channel	Total Revenue	Average Conversion Rate
Social Media	36376.18	0.03189

This PivotTable shows which channels generate the most revenue and which channels convert visitors most effectively. Comparing channels helps to determine whether performance issues are concentrated in one type of marketing activity.

The channel results show that Search Ads generate the highest total revenue, even though their conversion rate is only moderate, which suggests that this channel benefits from strong visitor volume rather than exceptional efficiency. Email produces less revenue overall but has the highest conversion rate, indicating that although fewer people arrive through Email, those who do are more likely to purchase. Social Media performs the weakest on both measures, with the lowest revenue and the lowest conversion rate, making it the most likely contributor to the overall decline in performance seen in the monthly summaries.

3.11.1.5.2 B. Summarize Performance by Region

1. Insert a second PivotTable using the same dataset.
2. Place Region in the Rows area.
3. Add Revenue (Sum) and Conversion Rate (Average) to the Values area again.

Table 3.11: Revenue and conversion rate by region

Region	Total Revenue	Average Conversion Rate
Rural	35524.68	0.04989
Suburban	41633.00	0.04533
Urban	43568.70	0.04044

This view highlights geographic differences. Some regions may have strong conversion rates but lower revenue, or vice versa. These differences are often hidden when all regions are combined into a single average.

The regional results reveal that Urban areas produce the most revenue but also have the lowest conversion rate, meaning Urban traffic is large but less efficient. Rural regions show the opposite pattern: they generate the least revenue but have the highest conversion rate, suggesting smaller but higher-quality traffic. Suburban regions fall between the two, with mid-range revenue and mid-range conversion efficiency. These differences show that regional performance varies for different reasons and that no single region is responsible for the overall trend.

3.11.1.6 Overall Diagnostic Conclusion

When the channel and region drilldowns are combined, the pattern becomes clear: the decline in revenue despite rising traffic is not caused by all channels or all regions equally. The primary weakness comes from Social Media, where both revenue and conversion rate are low, and from high-volume segments like Urban traffic, where efficiency is weakest. As a result, the business is attracting more visitors overall, but a growing share of that traffic is coming from lower-quality sources. This explains why revenue does not rise in step with visitor counts and points to traffic quality—not traffic quantity—as the central performance issue.

3.11.2 Practice

This practice dataset contains website performance data for Months 2, 7, and 11 across three marketing channels (Search Ads, Social Media, and Email) and three regions (Urban, Suburban, and Rural). For each combination of month, channel, and region, the dataset provides the number of website visitors, the conversion rate, and the average order value. Students will use these fields to calculate revenue, summarize performance by month, and analyze patterns across channels and regions to understand why results change over time.

Table 3.12: Marketing performance metrics for month 2

Month	Marketing Channel	Region	Website Visitors	Conversion Rate	Average Order Value
2	Search Ads	Urban	1650	0.048	70
2	Social Media	Urban	2250	0.034	67
...	...	...	...	...	...

3.11.2.1 Questions

1. Add a Revenue column by multiplying Website Visitors × Conversion Rate × Average Order Value for every row.
2. Create a PivotTable summarizing total Website Visitors, total Revenue, and average Conversion Rate by Month.
3. Identify one month where Website Visitors increased but Revenue did not increase.
4. Copy the monthly summary into a normal worksheet range and create a line chart showing Revenue by Month.
5. Create a second line chart showing Website Visitors by Month and compare the shapes of the two charts.

6. Calculate the correlation between Website Visitors and Revenue using the CORREL function.
7. Calculate the correlation between Conversion Rate and Revenue using the CORREL function.
8. Create a PivotTable by Marketing Channel showing total Revenue and average Conversion Rate for each channel.
9. Create a PivotTable by Region showing total Revenue and average Conversion Rate for each region.
10. Write a short conclusion explaining which channel or region appears to be contributing most to performance changes and why.

3.12 Lab 3-2 Root Cause Analysis

Root cause analysis is a core component of diagnostic analytics. While diagnostic analytics focuses on understanding why a performance change occurred, root cause analysis goes one step deeper by identifying the underlying drivers that are actually responsible for the problem—not just the symptoms that appear on the surface. In practice, this means testing assumptions, comparing multiple possible explanations, and using data to rule out factors that do not meaningfully contribute to the issue. In this lab, you will apply root cause analysis to a real operational scenario by examining patterns, relationships, and trends across several variables to determine which factors are most strongly linked to rising wait times. The goal is to move beyond guesses or intuition and use evidence to pinpoint the most likely cause of the problem.

3.12.1 Demonstration

A medical clinic has received complaints about long appointment wait times. Management believes the issue is caused by understaffing, but they want a data-based investigation before hiring new staff. You are provided with six months of operational data.

Table 3.13: Clinic operational performance metrics by month

Month	Avg Wait Time (min)	Appointments per Day	Staff on Duty	No-Show Rate (%)	System Downtime (hrs)
Jan	18	96	8	12	1.2
Feb	21	102	8	14	2.1
Mar	24	108	9	15	3.4
Apr	27	112	9	17	4.0
May	29	115	9	18	4.6

Month	Avg Wait Time (min)	Appointments per Day	Staff on Duty	No-Show Rate (%)	System Downtime (hrs)
Jun	31	118	9	19	5.2

3.12.1.1 Step 1: Chart average wait time by month

Begin by selecting the Month and Average Wait Time columns and inserting a standard line chart. This chart establishes the symptom pattern you are investigating: wait times rise steadily from January through June. Identifying the shape of the problem is the first step in root cause analysis, because it shows when the issue begins, how quickly it worsens, and whether the trend is consistent over time. Once the symptom is clearly visualized, you can compare it against other operational factors to determine which ones follow a similar pattern and may be contributing to the increase.

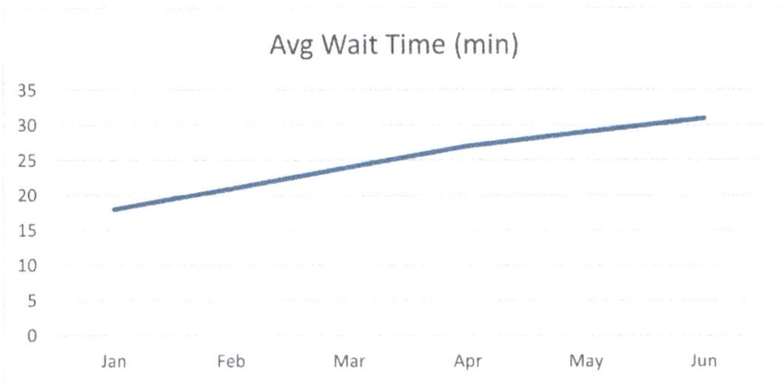

3.12.1.2 Step 2: Create Scatter Plots to Test Possible Causes

Next, create scatter plots to examine whether any operational factors move in a way that could plausibly explain the rise in wait times. Scatter plots are essential in root cause analysis because they reveal whether two variables change together in a consistent pattern. By comparing the shape and direction of each relationship, you can begin to determine which factors are aligned with the increasing wait times and which factors are unlikely to be contributing to the problem.

Build three separate charts: Wait Time vs. Appointments per Day, Wait Time vs. Staff on Duty, and Wait Time vs. System Downtime.

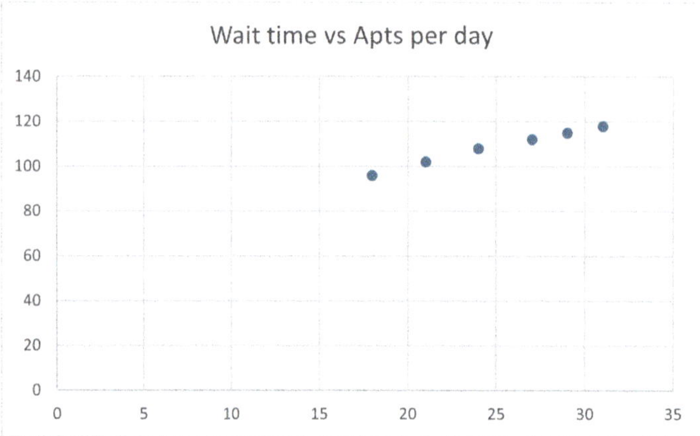

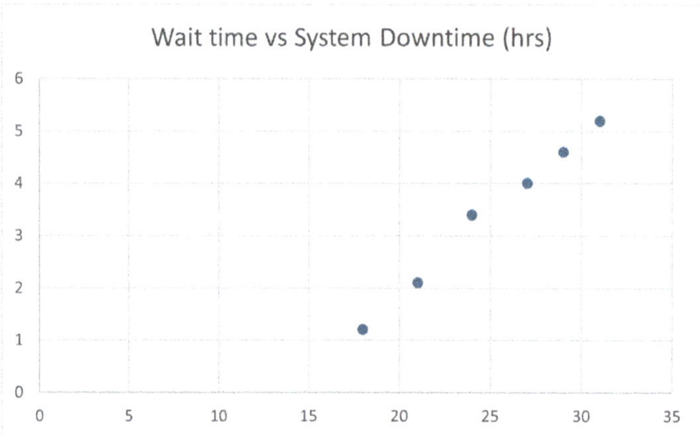

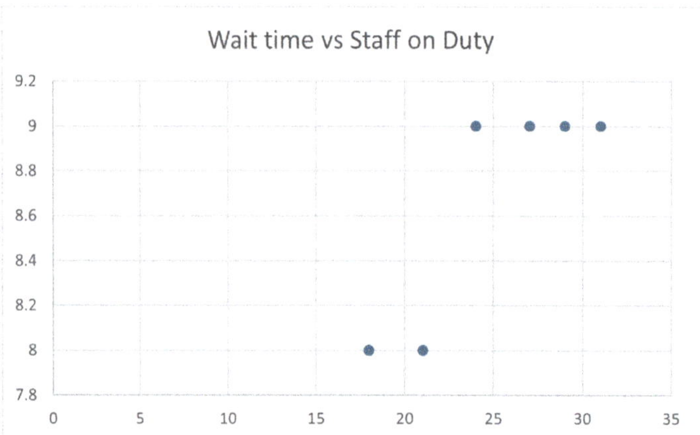

3.12.1.3 Step 3: Quantify Each Relationship with Correlations

After visually examining the scatter plots, use Excel's CORREL function to measure the strength of each relationship numerically. Calculate the correlation between wait time and each potential contributing factor: Appointments per Day, Staff on Duty, and System Downtime. Correlation values help determine whether a factor is strongly aligned with the rising wait times or only loosely related. This step is essential in root cause analysis because it provides evidence that supports or rules out possible explanations, allowing you to focus on the factors most likely driving the increase in wait times.

Table 3.14: Correlation between clinic wait time and operational factors

Variable Compared to Wait Time	Correlation (R)
Appointments per Day	0.86247
Staff on Duty	0.86247
System Downtime	0.99553

3.12.1.4 Step 4: Interpret the Evidence

The data shows that appointments per day increase each month, but the relationship with wait time is only moderately aligned, suggesting that higher patient volume contributes somewhat but does not fully explain the trend. Staffing levels increase slightly in March and then remain constant, while wait times continue rising, indicating that staffing is not the primary driver of the problem. In contrast, system downtime increases sharply and consistently across all six months, closely mirroring the upward pattern in wait times. This strong visual alignment, combined with the high correlation between downtime and wait time, points to system downtime as the factor most strongly associated with longer wait times. Based on the combined evidence, the most plausible root cause is the clinic's increasing system downtime, not understaffing.

3.12.2 Practice

This practice dataset contains six months of performance metrics for a single retail store that is experiencing declining sales, even though the company as a whole remains stable. The data includes several operational factors that could influence store performance: total monthly sales, customer foot traffic, average transaction value, staffing levels, and the number of inventory stockouts. Together, these variables allow you to investigate whether the sales decline is driven by fewer customers entering the store, changes in customer spending behavior, reduced staffing, or increasing inventory shortages. By comparing how each factor changes from January through June, you can begin identifying which trends align most closely with the drop in sales and which factors are unlikely to be contributing to the problem.

3.12.3 Table pt 1: Monthly retail performance metrics (Sales & Demand)

Month	Total Sales	Customer Foot Traffic	Avg Transaction Value ($)
Jan	182000	4200	43.30
Feb	176500	4150	42.50

Month	Total Sales	Customer Foot Traffic	Avg Transaction Value ($)
Mar	169800	4000	42.10
Apr	162300	3850	42.20
May	158700	3720	42.70
Jun	151900	3600	42.20

3.12.4 Table pt 2: Monthly retail operations metrics (Staffing & Supply)

Month	Staff Scheduled	Inventory Stockouts
Jan	14	6
Feb	14	8
Mar	13	11
Apr	13	14
May	13	16
Jun	12	19

3.12.4.1 Questions

1. Create a line chart showing Total Sales by Month.
2. Describe the pattern you see in the Total Sales line chart.
3. Create a scatter plot comparing Total Sales and Customer Foot Traffic.
4. Create a scatter plot comparing Total Sales and Avg Transaction Value.
5. Create a scatter plot comparing Total Sales and Inventory Stockouts.
6. Use the CORREL function to calculate the correlation between Total Sales and Customer Foot Traffic.
7. Use the CORREL function to calculate the correlation between Total Sales and Inventory Stockouts.
8. Use the CORREL function to calculate the correlation between Total Sales and Avg Transaction Value.
9. Based on the scatter plots and correlations, identify which factor appears most strongly related to the decline in sales and explain why.

Chapter 4

Forecasting

4.1 Learning Outcomes

4-1. Recognize basic patterns in business data that help predict the future

4-2. Understand simple methods businesses use to make predictions

4-3. Identify how computers help businesses make better forecasts

4-4. Recognize how businesses use forecasting to plan for inventory, staffing, and budgets

4.2 Introduction

Imagine you own a small ice cream shop, and it's March. Your ice cream supplier calls and asks, "How many gallons of vanilla ice cream should I deliver to you each week

this summer?" This seems like a simple question, but to answer it well, you need to predict how many customers will want vanilla ice cream over the next several months. You'll need to think about things like weather patterns, school schedules, local events, and how much vanilla you sold last summer.

This everyday business challenge shows what forecasting is all about. Every business, from the smallest corner store to the largest companies, must make decisions based on predictions about what will happen in the future. Will more customers visit next month? How much product should we order? How many employees will we need during busy times? These questions all require forecasting - using information we have today to make educated guesses about tomorrow.

Forecasting is like building a bridge between what we know happened in the past and what we need to plan for in the future. In previous modules, we learned how descriptive analytics tells us what happened, and diagnostic analytics helps us understand why it happened. Forecasting takes the next step by helping us predict what might happen next.

Think of forecasting like checking the weather forecast before planning a picnic. The weather service looks at current conditions and past weather patterns to predict whether it will rain tomorrow. They can't be 100% certain, but their prediction helps you decide whether to plan an outdoor event or choose an indoor activity instead. Business forecasting works the same way - it helps companies make better decisions even though the future is uncertain.

The value of good forecasting is enormous for businesses. Companies that are good at predicting future demand can keep just the right amount of products in stock - enough to satisfy customers without wasting money on items that sit unsold. They can schedule the right number of employees - enough to provide good service without paying for workers who have nothing to do. They can plan their budgets more accurately and avoid unpleasant surprises.

Modern technology has made forecasting much more powerful and accessible. Computer programs can now look at huge amounts of information and spot patterns that humans might miss. However, the basic principles of forecasting remain the same: look for patterns in what happened before, understand what causes those patterns, and use that knowledge to make informed predictions about the future.

Throughout this module, we'll explore how businesses use forecasting to plan for the future. We'll learn to recognize basic patterns in data that changes over time, understand simple methods for making predictions, see how computers help improve forecasting, and discover how businesses apply forecasting to real challenges like managing inventory, scheduling employees, and planning budgets.

Whether you're helping a small business plan for next month or working for a large company that needs to predict next year's performance, understanding forecasting will help you make better decisions and contribute more effectively to business success.

4.3 Recognizing Patterns That Help Predict the Future

4.3.1 Understanding Data That Changes Over Time

When businesses collect information over time - like daily sales, monthly customers, or yearly revenue - they create what's called time series data. This type of information is special because the order matters. Unlike other types of data where you might mix up the information randomly, time series data tells a story that unfolds over time, and that story contains valuable clues about what might happen next.

Think about your own daily routine. You probably wake up at roughly the same time each day, eat meals at predictable hours, and go to bed around the same time each night. If someone tracked your activities over several weeks, they would see patterns that repeat daily. Businesses have similar patterns in their data - some things happen predictably at certain times of day, week, month, or year.

Understanding these patterns is like learning to read the rhythm of a business. A coffee shop might notice that they sell more coffee on Monday mornings than Friday afternoons. A clothing store might see that winter coat sales are highest in October and November. An online store might observe that website visits are highest during lunch hours and evenings. These patterns aren't random - they reflect how customers behave and when they make purchasing decisions.

The key to successful forecasting is recognizing that most business data contains three main types of patterns: trends, seasonal patterns, and random ups and downs. Learning to identify these patterns is like learning to recognize different instruments in a band - once you can hear each part separately, you can better understand how they work together to create the overall performance.

4.3.2 Recognizing Trends in Business Data

A trend is the general direction that data moves over time. Think of it like the overall slope of a hill - it might go up, down, or stay relatively flat. In business, trends often reflect fundamental changes in the market, customer preferences, or company performance.

An upward trend might show a growing business, increasing customer satisfaction, or rising demand for a product. For example, a streaming service like Netflix might see a steady upward trend in the number of subscribers as more people discover their shows and decide to sign up. This trend reflects the growing popularity of streaming entertainment and the company's success in attracting customers.

A downward trend might indicate declining sales, decreasing market share, or changing customer preferences. A traditional bookstore might see a downward trend in physical book sales as more customers switch to e-books and online shopping. Understanding this trend helps the business owner decide whether to adapt their business model or find new ways to attract customers.

A flat trend suggests stability - the business is maintaining consistent performance over time. A local grocery store in a stable neighborhood might see relatively flat trends in overall sales, with small ups and downs around a consistent average level. This stability can be valuable for planning and budgeting.

It's important to remember that trends don't continue forever. A rapidly growing startup might see explosive growth in its early years, but that growth rate will eventually slow as the market matures. A declining business might stabilize at a lower level or find ways to reverse the trend through innovation or strategic changes.

4.3.3 Understanding Seasonal Patterns

Seasonal patterns are regular, predictable changes that happen at specific times. These patterns can occur daily, weekly, monthly, or yearly, and they often reflect natural human behavior, weather changes, or cultural events.

Daily seasonal patterns are common in many businesses. Restaurants typically see lunch and dinner rushes, with slower periods in between. Gas stations might be busiest during morning and evening commute times. Online stores often see higher website traffic during lunch hours when people browse from work, and in the evenings when people shop from home.

Weekly patterns reflect how people's routines change throughout the week. Movie theaters are typically busiest on Friday and Saturday nights. Business-to-business companies might see higher activity Tuesday through Thursday when people are focused on work. Retail stores often see increased traffic on weekends when people have more time to shop.

Monthly patterns might reflect payroll cycles, billing cycles, or monthly planning activities. Many consumers do their major shopping early in the month after receiving paychecks. Utility companies see predictable patterns in monthly usage based on weather and seasonal activities.

Yearly seasonal patterns are often the most dramatic and important for business planning. Retail businesses see major spikes during holiday shopping seasons. Tax preparation services are extremely busy from January through April. Lawn care companies see peak demand during spring and summer months. Understanding these patterns helps businesses prepare for busy periods and manage slower times.

4.3.4 A Simple Example: Ice Cream Shop Sales

Let's look at how these patterns work together using data from our ice cream shop example. Here's what the monthly sales might look like over two years:

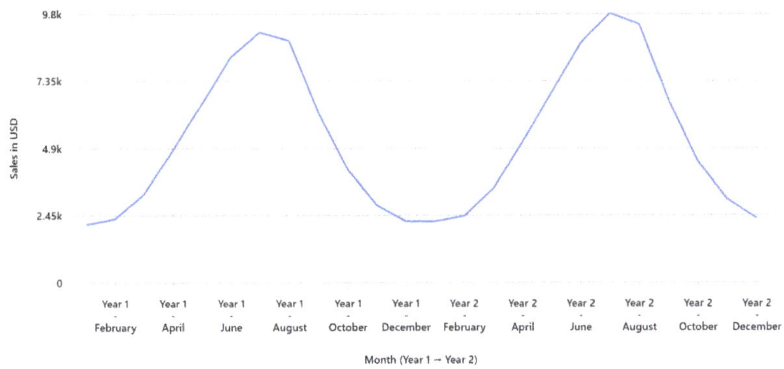

Data:

Month	Year 1 Sales	Year 2 Sales
January	2100	2200
February	2300	2400
March	3200	3400
April	4800	5100
May	6500	6900
June	8200	8700
July	9100	9800
August	8800	9400
September	6200	6600
October	4100	4400
November	2800	3000
December	2200	2300

Looking at this data, we can see several clear patterns:

Seasonal Pattern: Sales are highest during summer months (June, July, August) and lowest during winter months (January, February, December). This makes perfect sense - people eat more ice cream when it's hot outside.

Trend: Comparing Year 1 to Year 2, we can see that sales increased in every month. The average monthly sales went from about $5,000 in Year 1 to about $5,300 in Year 2, showing a positive growth trend of about 6%.

Combined Effect: The seasonal pattern and growth trend work together. July had the highest sales in both years, but July in Year 2 was higher than July in Year1 because of the overall growth trend.

Understanding these patterns helps the ice cream shop owner make better decisions. They know to order more inventory and schedule more employees during summer months. They can plan for slower winter periods by reducing costs or finding ways to attract customers with winter-friendly products. The growth trend suggests the business is healthy and might justify investments in expansion or improvements.

4.3.5 Random Ups and Downs

Even after accounting for trends and seasonal patterns, business data still contains random fluctuations - unpredictable ups and downs that can't be explained by regular patterns. These fluctuations are normal and expected, but understanding them is important for realistic forecasting.

Random fluctuations might be caused by weather (an unusually hot day brings more ice cream customers), local events (a festival brings extra visitors to town), economic factors (people have more or less spending money), or countless other unpredictable influences. The key is recognizing that these fluctuations are part of normal business operations.

Smart business owners learn to distinguish between normal random fluctuations and significant changes that might indicate new trends or problems. If ice cream sales are unusually low for one day, that's probably just a random fluctuation. But if sales are consistently lower for several weeks, that might indicate a new trend that requires investigation and response.

Understanding random fluctuations also helps set realistic expectations for forecasting accuracy. No forecasting method can predict random events, so perfect predictions are impossible. Good forecasting aims to capture the predictable patterns while acknowledging that actual results will vary around the predictions due to random factors.

4.4 Simple Methods for Making Predictions

4.4.1 The Moving Average: Learning from Recent Experience

One of the simplest and most intuitive ways to predict the future is to look at what happened recently and assume that pattern will continue. The moving average method does exactly this by calculating the average of the most recent data points and using that average as the prediction for the next period.

Think of a moving average like asking several friends about their recent experiences at a restaurant before deciding whether to eat there yourself. If the last five people who ate there all had good experiences, you'd probably expect to have a good experience too. The moving average works the same way with business data - it assumes that recent performance is the best indicator of near-future performance.

Here's how it works with our ice cream shop example. Let's say we want to predict sales for next month using a 3-month moving average. We would take the sales from the last three months, add them up, and divide by three:

Example Calculation:

- August sales: \$9,400
- September sales: \$6,600
- October sales: \$4,400
- 3-month moving average = (\$9,400 + \$6,600 + \$4,400) ÷ 3 = \$6,800

So our prediction for November would be \$6,800.

The number of months you include in the moving average makes a big difference. A shorter moving average (like 3 months) responds quickly to recent changes but might be influenced by random fluctuations. A longer moving average (like 12 months) is more stable but might be slow to detect new trends.

For our ice cream shop, a 3-month moving average might work well during stable periods, but it would have problems during seasonal transitions. As we move from summer to fall, the 3-month average would still include high summer sales, making the prediction too optimistic for fall months.

4.4.2 Adjusting for Seasonal Patterns

Since many businesses have strong seasonal patterns, we need forecasting methods that can account for these regular changes. One simple approach is to use seasonal averages - looking at what typically happens during the same period in previous years.

For seasonal forecasting, we might calculate what usually happens in each month by averaging across multiple years. Using our ice cream shop data:

November Seasonal Average:

- November Year 1: \$2,800
- November Year 2: \$3,000
- November average: (\$2,800 + \$3,000) ÷ 2 = \$2,900

This seasonal approach would predict November sales of \$2,900, which is much more realistic than the \$6,800 prediction from the simple moving average.

We can make this even better by combining seasonal patterns with trend information. If we notice that sales have been growing by about 6% per year, we might adjust our seasonal prediction upward to account for this growth:

Trend-Adjusted Seasonal Prediction: November seasonal average: \$2,900 Growth adjustment (6%): \$2,900 × 1.06 = \$3,074

This gives us a prediction of about \$3,074 for November, which accounts for both the seasonal pattern and the growth trend.

4.4.3 Simple Trend Forecasting

When data shows a clear trend over time, we can use that trend to make predictions about the future. The simplest approach is to draw a straight line through the historical data and extend that line into the future.

Let's look at the total annual sales for our ice cream shop:

- Year 1 total: $60,100
- Year 2 total: $63,700
- Annual growth: $3,600

If this growth continues, we might predict:

- Year 3 total: $63,700 + $3,600 = $67,300

We can break this down to monthly predictions by combining the trend with seasonal patterns. If we expect Year 3 total sales of $67,300, and we know that July typically represents about 15% of annual sales, we might predict July Year 3 sales of about $10,100.

This approach works well when trends are stable and predictable. However, trends can change due to competition, economic conditions, or other factors. Smart forecasters regularly check whether historical trends are still valid and adjust their predictions accordingly.

4.4.4 Combining Different Methods

Often, the best forecasting approach combines multiple simple methods rather than relying on just one. This is like getting a second opinion from a doctor - different methods might provide different perspectives that together give a more complete picture.

For example, we might create three different predictions for November ice cream sales:

1. 3-month moving average: $6,800 (too high, doesn't account for seasonality)
2. Seasonal average: $2,900 (accounts for seasonality but ignores recent growth)
3. Trend-adjusted seasonal: $3,074 (accounts for both seasonality and growth)

We might then combine these predictions by taking their average, or we might weight them based on which method has been most accurate in the past. The combined forecast might be more reliable than any single method alone.

4.4.5 A Real Forecasting Example: Monthly Sales Prediction

Let's work through a complete example using 24 months of sales data for a small retail business:

Month	Sales	3-Month MA	Seasonal Index	Trend-Adjusted Forecast
Jan Y1	15200	-	0.85	-
Feb Y1	16800	-	0.94	-
Mar Y1	18500	-	1.03	-

Month	Sales	3-Month MA	Seasonal Index	Trend-Adjusted Forecast
Apr Y1	17200	16833	0.96	-
May Y1	19100	17533	1.07	-
Jun Y1	20300	18600	1.13	-
Jul Y1	21800	19133	1.22	-
Aug Y1	20900	20733	1.17	-
Sep Y1	18600	20433	1.04	-
Oct Y1	16400	18633	0.92	-
Nov Y1	14200	16400	0.79	-
Dec Y1	22100	17567	1.23	-
Jan Y2	16100	17600	0.85	16320
Feb Y2	17900	18700	0.94	18048
Mar Y2	19800	17933	1.03	19776

The table shows how different forecasting methods work:

3-Month Moving Average: Takes the average of the previous three months. Simple but doesn't account for seasonal patterns.

Seasonal Index: Shows how each month typically compares to the annual average. January has an index of 0.85, meaning it's typically 15% below average.

Trend-Adjusted Forecast: Combines the seasonal pattern with the overall growth trend to make more accurate predictions.

Looking at the forecasts versus actual results:

- January Y2 actual: \$16,100, forecast: $16,320 (error: -220)$
- February Y2 actual: \$17,900, forecast: $18,048 (error: -148)$
- March Y2 actual: \$19,800, forecast: $19,776 (error: +24)$

The trend-adjusted seasonal forecast performs quite well, with small errors that are typical for business forecasting.

4.4.6 Understanding Forecast Accuracy

No forecast is perfect, and understanding the typical size of forecasting errors helps set realistic expectations. In our retail example, the forecasts were off by \$148 to \$220, which represents errors of about 1-2% of actual sales. This level of accuracy is quite good for business forecasting.

Different businesses and situations require different levels of forecasting accuracy. A grocery store forecasting demand for perishable items needs very accurate short-term forecasts to minimize waste. A manufacturing company planning production capacity might accept less precise forecasts if they're planning far enough ahead to make adjustments.

The key is understanding the cost of forecasting errors. Overestimating demand might lead to excess inventory and storage costs. Underestimating demand might result in stockouts and lost sales. The best forecasting approach balances these costs while providing predictions that are accurate enough for effective decision-making.

4.5 How Computers Help Make Better Predictions

4.5.1 The Rise of Smart Forecasting Systems

Just as calculators made math faster and more accurate, computers have revolutionized business forecasting by handling complex calculations and analyzing large amounts of data much faster than humans ever could. Modern forecasting software can examine years of historical data, test dozens of different prediction methods, and automatically choose the approach that works best for each specific situation.

Think of computer-assisted forecasting like having a very smart assistant who never gets tired and can remember every detail from years of business data. While a human analyst might look at a few months of sales data and make educated guesses about patterns, a computer can analyze every day of the past five years, consider dozens of factors that might influence sales, and test hundreds of different forecasting approaches to find the most accurate one.

The real power of computer forecasting isn't just speed - it's the ability to spot patterns that humans might miss. A person looking at daily sales data might notice that Fridays are usually busy, but a computer might discover that Fridays are especially busy when it's sunny, or when payday falls on Thursday, or when there's a local sports game that evening. These subtle patterns can significantly improve forecasting accuracy.

However, computers don't replace human judgment - they enhance it. The best forecasting systems combine computer analysis with human understanding of the business. A computer might predict that ice cream sales will be high next Tuesday based on weather forecasts and historical patterns, but a human manager knows that the main street will be closed for construction, which might reduce foot traffic and sales.

4.5.2 Automatic Pattern Detection

One of the biggest advantages of computer forecasting is automatic pattern detection. Instead of requiring a human analyst to manually examine data and identify trends and seasonal patterns, modern software can automatically discover these patterns and adjust forecasting methods accordingly.

For example, a computer analyzing restaurant sales data might automatically detect:

- Daily patterns (lunch and dinner rushes)

- Weekly patterns (busier weekends)
- Monthly patterns (higher sales around paydays)
- Seasonal patterns (outdoor seating more popular in summer)
- Holiday effects (special patterns around major holidays)
- Weather sensitivity (how temperature and precipitation affect sales)

The computer can then create forecasting models that account for all these patterns simultaneously, something that would be extremely difficult for a human to do manually. As new data becomes available, the system can automatically update its understanding of these patterns and adjust future predictions accordingly.

This automatic pattern detection is particularly valuable for businesses with complex data. A large retail chain with hundreds of stores might have different patterns at each location based on local demographics, competition, and economic conditions. Computer systems can automatically identify and account for these location-specific patterns without requiring individual analysis of each store.

4.5.3 Machine Learning for Business Forecasting

Machine learning represents the next level of computer-assisted forecasting. While traditional computer forecasting uses predetermined rules and formulas, machine learning systems can actually learn from experience and improve their predictions over time.

Think of machine learning like teaching a computer to recognize patterns the same way you might teach a child to recognize different types of dogs. You show the child many examples of different dogs, pointing out the features that distinguish breeds. Eventually, the child learns to identify breeds on their own, even for dogs they've never seen before. Machine learning works similarly - you show the computer lots of examples of business data and outcomes, and it learns to identify patterns that predict future results.

A machine learning system forecasting retail sales might learn that:

- Sales increase when competitor prices go up
- Certain weather patterns lead to higher demand for specific products
- Social media mentions correlate with future sales spikes
- Economic indicators predict changes in customer spending patterns

The system discovers these relationships automatically by analyzing historical data, and it can continuously refine its understanding as new information becomes available. This means the forecasting system gets smarter over time, adapting to changing business conditions and improving its accuracy.

4.5.4 Real-Time Forecasting and Automatic Updates

Traditional forecasting often involved creating predictions once per month or quarter and using those predictions until the next forecasting cycle. Modern computer systems can update forecasts continuously as new information becomes available, providing much more current and accurate predictions.

For example, an e-commerce company might update its sales forecasts every hour based on:

- Current website traffic patterns
- Real-time competitor pricing
- Social media sentiment
- Weather forecasts
- Economic news
- Inventory levels

This real-time updating allows businesses to respond quickly to changing conditions. If a sudden weather change is likely to increase demand for certain products, the system can immediately update forecasts and trigger automatic reordering to ensure adequate inventory.

Automatic updating also helps businesses avoid the problems that occur when forecasts become outdated. In rapidly changing markets, a forecast created last month might be completely irrelevant today. Real-time systems ensure that decisions are always based on the most current predictions available.

4.5.5 AI-Powered Forecasting Examples

Retail Chain Example: A clothing retailer uses machine learning to forecast demand for each product at each store location. The system considers historical sales patterns for similar items, current fashion trends from social media, local weather forecasts, regional economic conditions, competitor pricing and promotions, and store-specific customer demographics. Based on these insights, the AI automatically adjusts orders for each store, keeping popular items in stock while reducing excess inventory of slower-selling products.

Restaurant Chain Example: A fast-food chain uses AI to predict hourly customer demand at each location. The system analyzes historical traffic patterns, local event schedules, weather forecasts, school calendars, traffic conditions, and social media mentions. This allows the restaurants to optimize staffing and food preparation, reducing wait times and minimizing food waste.

Online Service Example: A streaming service applies machine learning to forecast server capacity needs. It examines historical usage patterns, content release schedules, seasonal viewing trends, marketing campaign timing, competitor activities, and global events that could affect viewership. This ensures the service can handle peak demand efficiently without over-investing in unnecessary server capacity.

4.5.6 Understanding AI Forecasting Results

While AI-powered forecasting can be highly accurate, these systems often function like "black boxes," producing predictions without showing exactly how they arrived at them. Modern AI tools address this by providing explanations alongside forecasts, such as attributing a sales increase to favorable weather, competitor price changes, historical seasonal patterns, or social media sentiment. These insights help managers understand the reasoning behind predictions, assess their reliability, and determine when human judgment should override AI recommendations.

4.5.7 Limitations and Considerations

Despite their power, AI forecasting systems have important limitations that businesses need to understand. These systems are only as good as the data they're trained on, and they can struggle with situations that are very different from historical patterns.

For example, the COVID-19 pandemic created business conditions that were completely unlike anything in historical data. Many AI forecasting systems that had been very accurate suddenly became unreliable because they had never "learned" how to handle such dramatic and sudden changes in customer behavior.

AI systems can also be fooled by coincidental patterns in data. If ice cream sales happened to be high every time a particular sports team won games, an AI system might incorrectly learn that sports results predict ice cream demand. Human oversight is important to catch these kinds of spurious relationships.

The best approach combines AI capabilities with human judgment. AI systems excel at processing large amounts of data and identifying complex patterns, while humans provide business context, common sense, and the ability to recognize when unusual circumstances require different approaches.

4.6 Using Forecasting for Business Planning

4.6.1 Inventory Management

One of the most important applications of forecasting in business is inventory management - figuring out how much of each product to keep in stock. This might seem simple, but it's actually a delicate balancing act. Too little inventory means disappointed customers and lost sales. Too much inventory ties up money and storage space, and products might become obsolete or spoil before they can be sold.

Think about a grocery store trying to decide how many gallons of milk to order for next week. If they order too little, they'll run out and customers will go to competitors. If they order too much, some milk will expire and have to be thrown away, wasting money. The store needs to predict how much milk customers will buy, accounting for factors like weather (people buy more milk before snowstorms), holidays (different consumption patterns), and local events (a school festival might bring more families to the area).

Forecasting helps solve this problem by predicting future demand so businesses can order the right amount of inventory. Different types of products require different forecasting approaches. Fast-moving items like bread or milk need daily forecasting to avoid stockouts. Seasonal items like winter coats or swimsuits need longer-term forecasting to ensure adequate supply during peak seasons. Expensive items like electronics need careful forecasting because the cost of excess inventory is high.

Let's look at a simple example of how a small electronics store might use forecasting for inventory management:

Month	Units Sold	Forecast Next Month	Order Quantity
January	45	48	50

Month	Units Sold	Forecast Next Month	Order Quantity
February	52	49	52
March	47	50	53
April	55	51	54
May	49	52	55
June	58	54	57

The store uses forecasting to predict next month's sales, then orders slightly more than the forecast to provide a safety buffer. This approach helps ensure they don't run out of popular models while avoiding excessive inventory.

4.6.2 Staffing and Scheduling: Having the Right People at the Right Time

Just like inventory management, staffing requires businesses to predict future needs and plan accordingly. Too few employees means poor customer service and overworked staff. Too many employees means unnecessary labor costs that reduce profitability.

Staffing forecasts need to consider multiple factors that affect how many employees are needed. A restaurant needs more servers during dinner rush hours and fewer during slow afternoon periods. A retail store needs more cashiers during weekend shopping periods and holiday seasons. A call center needs more representatives during business hours and fewer during nights and weekends.

Consider how a small restaurant might use forecasting for staff scheduling:

Day	Forecasted Customers	Servers Needed	Kitchen Staff Needed
Monday	120	3	2
Tuesday	135	3	2
Wednesday	140	4	2
Thursday	160	4	3
Friday	220	6	4
Saturday	250	7	4
Sunday	180	5	3

The restaurant uses customer forecasts to determine how many employees to schedule each day. This helps ensure good service during busy periods while controlling labor costs during slower times.

Seasonal staffing presents additional challenges. Many businesses need to hire temporary employees for busy seasons. A tax preparation service needs extra staff from January through April. A landscaping company needs more workers during spring and summer. Retail stores need additional employees during holiday shopping seasons.

Effective seasonal staffing requires long-term forecasting to predict when additional employees will be needed and how many to hire. It also requires planning for training time, since new employees need time to learn their jobs before they become fully productive.

4.6.3 Financial Planning and Budgeting

Forecasting plays a crucial role in financial planning and budgeting by helping businesses predict future revenues and expenses. This enables better cash flow management, more accurate budget preparation, and more informed investment decisions.

Revenue forecasting helps businesses predict how much money they'll earn in future periods. This information is essential for planning expenses, determining whether the business can afford new investments, and ensuring adequate cash flow to meet obligations.

Let's look at how a small consulting business might use forecasting for financial planning:

Quarter	Historical Revenue	Forecasted Revenue	Confidence Level
Q1 2025	85000	88000	High
Q2 2025	92000	95000	High
Q3 2025	78000	82000	Medium
Q4 2025	96000	100000	Medium

The business uses historical data and current market conditions to forecast future revenue. The confidence levels help indicate how reliable each forecast is likely to be. Q1 and Q2 forecasts might be more reliable because they're based on existing client contracts, while Q3 and Q4 forecasts are less certain because they depend on winning new business.

Expense forecasting helps businesses predict future costs and plan accordingly. Some expenses are relatively predictable (rent, insurance, salaries), while others vary with business activity (materials, shipping, commissions). Understanding these patterns helps create more accurate budgets and identify potential cash flow problems before they occur.

4.6.4 Seasonal Business Planning

Many businesses experience significant seasonal variations that require special planning approaches. Understanding and forecasting these seasonal patterns is crucial for success in seasonal businesses.

A lawn care company provides a good example of seasonal business planning:

Month	Revenue % of Annual	Staffing Level	Equipment Needs
January	2	Minimal	Maintenance
February	3	Minimal	Preparation
March	8	Ramp up	Full deployment
April	15	Full staff	Peak capacity
May	18	Full staff	Peak capacity
June	16	Full staff	Peak capacity
July	14	Full staff	Peak capacity
August	12	Full staff	Peak capacity
September	8	Reduced	Partial capacity
October	3	Minimal	Winterization
November	1	Minimal	Storage
December	0	Minimal	Planning

This seasonal pattern requires careful planning throughout the year:

Winter Planning (December-February): Use slow season for equipment maintenance, staff training, and planning for the upcoming season. Develop marketing campaigns and prepare for spring hiring.

Spring Ramp-Up (March-April): Hire and train seasonal employees, deploy equipment, and begin active marketing to secure customers for the peak season.

Peak Season (May-August): Focus on service delivery and customer satisfaction. Monitor performance against forecasts and adjust operations as needed.

Fall Wind-Down (September-November): Complete final services, winterize equipment, and plan for the next year. Analyze performance and identify improvements for next season.

4.6.5 Practical Forecasting Implementation

Implementing forecasting in a small business doesn't require expensive software or complex statistical methods. Many businesses can start with simple approaches using basic spreadsheet tools.

Step 1: Collect Historical Data Gather at least 12-24 months of historical data for the metric you want to forecast (sales, customers, expenses, etc.). More data is generally better, but even a year of data can provide useful insights.

Step 2: Identify Patterns Look for trends (generally increasing or decreasing), seasonal patterns (regular changes at specific times), and unusual events that affected the data.

Step 3: Choose a Forecasting Method Start with simple methods like moving averages or seasonal averages. These are easy to understand and often work well for basic business forecasting.

Step 4: Make Forecasts Apply your chosen method to create forecasts for the next few periods. Start with short-term forecasts (1-3 months) which are generally more accurate than long-term predictions.

Step 5: Monitor and Adjust Compare your forecasts to actual results and adjust your methods based on what you learn. Forecasting is an iterative process that improves with experience.

Month	Actual Sales	3-Month Average	Seasonal Factor	Adjusted Forecast
Jan	12000	-	0.85	-
Feb	13500	-	0.95	-
Mar	15200	-	1.07	-
Apr	14800	13567	1.04	14110
May	16100	14500	1.13	16385
Jun	17300	16067	1.22	19602

This simple approach combines moving averages with seasonal adjustments to create more accurate forecasts than either method alone.

The key to successful business forecasting is starting simple and gradually improving your methods as you gain experience and understanding of your business patterns. Even basic forecasting is usually better than no forecasting, and the insights gained from the process often prove as valuable as the predictions themselves.

4.7 Conclusion

Forecasting and predictive analytics help businesses bridge the gap between past performance and future planning. By recognizing trends, seasonal patterns, and random fluctuations, businesses can make informed decisions about inventory, staffing, and budgets. Simple methods, like moving averages and seasonal averages, provide a solid starting point for predictions, while computers and AI enhance accuracy by processing large datasets and detecting complex patterns. Although forecasts are never perfect, combining analytical tools with human judgment ensures businesses are prepared for uncertainty and can respond effectively to changing conditions. Ultimately, mastering forecasting empowers organizations to optimize operations, improve customer satisfaction, and plan strategically for growth.

4.8 Key Terms

Forecasting: The process of using historical data and patterns to make informed predictions about future events in business.

Time Series Data: Data collected over time, where the order of observations matters, revealing trends and patterns.

Trend: The general direction of data over time, indicating growth, decline, or stability in a business metric.

Seasonal Pattern: Regular, predictable fluctuations in business data that occur at specific times, such as daily, weekly, monthly, or yearly.

Random Fluctuations: Unpredictable variations in data that cannot be explained by trends or seasonal patterns.

Moving Average: A simple forecasting method that predicts future values based on the average of recent data points.

Seasonal Average: A forecasting approach that accounts for regular seasonal patterns by averaging historical data for the same period over multiple years.

Trend-Adjusted Forecast: A method that combines both trend and seasonal patterns to make more accurate predictions.

AI-Powered Forecasting: Using artificial intelligence and machine learning to analyze large datasets, detect patterns, and generate forecasts, often with real-time updates.

Forecast Accuracy: A measure of how close predicted values are to actual outcomes, important for evaluating the reliability of forecasts.

4.9 Review Questions

1. What is the difference between a trend and a seasonal pattern in business data?
2. How does time series data help businesses make predictions?
3. Explain how random fluctuations can affect forecasting accuracy.
4. Describe how a moving average is calculated and when it might be most useful.
5. How can trend-adjusted seasonal forecasting improve prediction accuracy?
6. Give an example of how AI-powered forecasting can benefit a retail or service business.
7. Why is human judgment still important when using AI for forecasting?
8. Explain how forecasting can help with inventory management, staffing, and financial planning.

4.10 References

[1] Nielsen IQ. (2024). *AI-Powered Forecasting: A Beginner's Guide to the Future of*

Predictive Analytics. https://nielseniq.com/global/en/insights/commentary/2024/ai-powered-forecasting-a-beginners-guide-to-the-future-of-predictive-analytics/

[2] Bain & Company. (2024). *The Future of Financial Planning Is Autonomous*. https://www.bain.com/insights/the-future-of-financial-planning-is-autonomous

[3] AutoStore System. (2024). *Your Guide to Better Inventory Forecasting*. https://www.autostoresystem.com/insights/how-to-forecast-inventory

4.11 Lab 4-1 Trend Analysis and Forecasting

This lab focuses on identifying and interpreting overall trends in business data using Excel. You will analyze how values change over time and use linear trendlines to make simple forecasts based on historical patterns. The emphasis is on understanding the general direction of data (increasing, decreasing, or stable) and using that trend to project short-term future values. You may use AI tools such as ChatGPT to help interpret results, but all calculations and forecasts must be created and verified in Excel.

4.11.1 Demonstration

A small software company offers a monthly subscription service. Management wants to understand whether subscriber growth is accelerating, slowing down, or remaining steady so they can plan marketing spending and server capacity.

Table 4.8: Monthly subscriber growth for a software subscription service

Month	Subscribers (Year 1)	Subscribers (Year 2)
Jan	1240	1360
Feb	1285	1420
Mar	1330	1480
Apr	1390	1555
May	1460	1630
Jun	1520	1700
Jul	1590	1775
Aug	1645	1835
Sep	1700	1900
Oct	1755	1965
Nov	1810	2025
Dec	1860	2090

4.11.1.1 Step 1: Set Up Data in Excel

Begin by opening Excel and entering your data into a single table. Type Month in cell A1, Year 1 in B1, and Year 2 in C1, then list the months from January through December in column A and enter the corresponding values for each year in columns B and C. After entering the data, highlight the entire table so it is ready to be used for a chart.

4.11.1.2 Step 2: Create Line Chart

With the data selected, go to the Insert tab and choose a 2-D Line chart. Excel will automatically generate a chart that displays both Year 1 and Year 2 as separate lines across the months, allowing you to visually compare how the values change over time.

4.11.1.3 Step 3: Add Trendline for Year 1

To add a linear trendline for Year 1, click directly on the Year 1 line in the chart to select it, then right-click and choose "Add Trendline." In the panel that appears, select the Linear option and check the box labeled "Display Equation on chart" so that the regression equation is shown.

4.11.1.4 Step 4: Add Trendline for Year 2

Repeat the same process for Year 2 by clicking on the Year 2 line, right-clicking, and selecting "Add Trendline." Again, choose the Linear option and display the equation on the chart so that both years have visible trendline equations.

4.11.1.5 Step 5: Interpret Trendline Equations

Once both equations are displayed, observe that Excel is calculating a linear regression even though the chart is a line chart. It does this by treating each month as a numerical value from 1 to 12. The equation will appear in the form $y = mx + b$, where the slope (m) represents the average monthly increase. A larger slope indicates faster growth, while a smaller slope indicates slower growth.

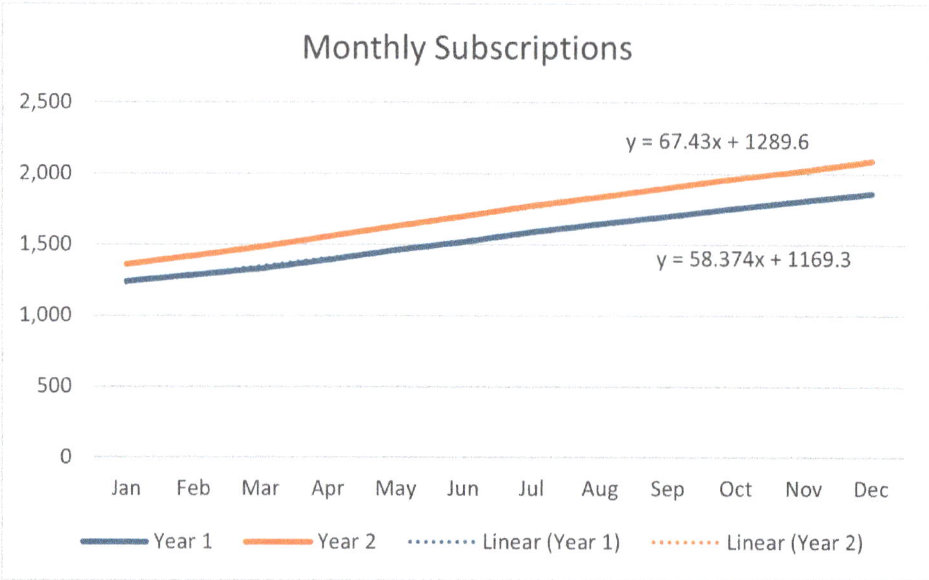

4.11.1.6 Step 6: Compare Growth Rates

Compare the slopes of the two equations to determine whether subscriber growth is increasing, decreasing, or staying consistent between the two years. This comparison is the main goal of the analysis. Year 2 seems to have accelerated growth rate.

4.11.1.7 Step 7: Create Forecast

To create a forecast, use the equation from Year 2 and substitute the next three-month values into the formula. Since December corresponds to 12, use 13 for January of the next year, 14 for February, and 15 for March, then calculate the resulting values to estimate future subscriber counts.

Table 4.9: Projected subscriber growth for Year 3

Month	Subscribers Forecast (Year 3)
Jan	2165
Feb	2233
Mar	2300
Apr	2368
May	2435
Jun	2502
Jul	2570
Aug	2637
Sep	2705
Oct	2772
Nov	2840

Month	Subscribers Forecast (Year 3)
Dec	2907

4.11.2 Practice

A sporting goods store sells outdoor equipment. Management wants to forecast demand for a popular product so they can plan inventory purchases for the next year.

Table 4.10: Monthly performance comparison between Year 1 and Year 2

Month	Metric (Year 1)	Metric (Year 2)
Jan	120	135
Feb	135	150
Mar	210	235
Apr	340	370
May	520	560
Jun	710	760
Jul	780	835
Aug	740	800
Sep	480	520
Oct	310	340
Nov	190	210
Dec	140	155

4.11.2.1 Questions

1. Enter the sales data into Excel and create a line chart showing Year 1 and Year 2 sales. What overall trend do you notice in the sales data?
2. Add a linear trendline to the Year 2 data and display the equation on the chart. What does the trendline suggest about sales growth over time?
3. Calculate the month-to-month sales changes for Year 2. Which months show the biggest increase and the biggest decrease in sales?
4. Identify the three highest-sales months and the three lowest-sales months in Year 2. What do these months tell you about seasonal demand?
5. Calculate a 3-month moving average for the Year 2 sales data. How does the moving average help show the overall sales trend more clearly?
6. Use the Year 2 trendline equation to forecast sales for January, February, and March of Year 3. What do your forecasts suggest about future demand?

7. Create a forecast for January, February, and March of Year 3 using the 3-month moving average method. How are these forecasts different from the trendline forecasts?

8. Compare the trendline forecast and the moving-average forecast. Which method do you think gives a more realistic prediction for this product, and why?

9. Describe the seasonal pattern shown in the sales data. How could this pattern affect inventory planning for the next year?

4.12 Lab 4-2 Combined Forecasting

In this lab, you will learn how businesses make more realistic forecasts by combining two important patterns found in data: long-term trends and seasonal changes. Most real-world business data is not random—it usually shows a general direction over time (trend) and repeated patterns that happen every year (seasonality), such as higher sales during holidays or slower months during off-seasons.

Instead of relying on a single forecasting method, you will practice using multiple approaches in Excel, including moving averages, seasonal indexing, and trend-based calculations. You will then compare these methods to see how each one performs and how combining them can produce more accurate predictions.

The goal of this lab is not just to calculate numbers, but to understand how businesses use data to make decisions about inventory, staffing, budgeting, and planning for future demand. You will also see how AI tools can support forecasting by helping interpret results, while still requiring you to perform all calculations in Excel.

By the end of this lab, you should be able to take historical sales data and build a reasonable forecast for the next year using both trend and seasonal information.

4.12.1 Demonstration

We are working with monthly sales data from a small retail store over two years (24 months). The goal is to forecast sales for Year 3. This data contains seasonal patterns, trends, and random fluctuations.

Table 4.11: Monthly sales comparison between Year 1 and Year 2

Month	Year 1 Sales	Year 2 Sales
Jan	15200	16100
Feb	16800	17900
Mar	18500	19800
Apr	17200	18200
May	19100	20300

Month	Year 1 Sales	Year 2 Sales
Jun	20300	21600
Jul	21800	23000
Aug	20900	22100
Sep	18600	19800
Oct	16400	17500
Nov	14200	15300
Dec	22100	23400

4.12.1.1 Step 1: Restructure data in long format

For forecasting methods such as moving averages, data is arranged as a continuous time series so that each value reflects sequential time order across both years. Copy your data into a new Excel sheet and arrange it as a single continuous time series with three columns: Time Period (1–24), Month (Jan–Dec repeated), and Sales. Enter Year 1 first (periods 1–12) followed by Year 2 (periods 13–24) so Excel treats the data as one continuous timeline for forecasting calculations. The first two rows are displayed below.

Table 4.12: Monthly sales for Year 1 by time period

Time Period	Month	Sales
1	Jan	15200
2	Feb	16800

4.12.1.2 Step 2: Calculating a 3-Month Moving Average

A 3-month moving average is a simple way to smooth out ups and downs in the data. Instead of looking at just one month (which can be high or low for random reasons), we average the last three months to get a more stable picture of the trend. This helps us see the underlying pattern more clearly and make better short-term forecasts.

In Excel, you will use the formula:

=AVERAGE(previous three months)

To estimate sales for March (Year 1), take the average of January, February, and March of Year 1: (15,200 + 16,800 + 18,500) ÷ 3 = 16,833.

You will continue this same process for each month, starting with April, by always averaging the previous three months of data. Table: Monthly sales with 3-month moving average

Time Period	Month	Sales	3-Month Moving Average
1	Jan	15200	
2	Feb	16800	
3	Mar	18500	16833
…	…	…	…
24	Dec	23400	18733

4.12.1.3 Step 3: Calculating Seasonal Index

In the previous step, we used a 3-month moving average to identify the overall trend in sales, which shows the general direction of the business over time (whether sales are increasing, decreasing, or staying steady). However, that trend does not explain why some months are always higher or lower than others.

In real business data, sales are often affected by seasonal patterns, meaning certain months consistently perform better or worse every year (for example, holiday months or slow summer periods). To measure this pattern, we calculate the seasonal index, which tells us how each month compares to a normal average month.

The seasonal index helps us adjust our forecast so it reflects not just the overall trend, but also the predictable ups and downs that happen every year.

Compute average sales for each month across both years: Example for January:

(15,200 + 16,100) ÷ 2 = 15,650

The seasonal index is calculated by first finding each month's average sales across the two years, which is done by adding the Year 1 and Year 2 sales for that month and dividing by 2. Next, you calculate the overall average sales across all months (the average of the 12 monthly averages). The overall average sales across all months is calculated by first finding the average sales for each month across the two years, then averaging those 12 monthly values together. For this dataset, the overall average monthly sales is approximately 18,921 units.

Finally, each month's seasonal index is found by dividing that month's average sales by the overall average. This shows whether a month typically performs above or below a normal month.

Month Seasonal Index = Month Sales ÷ Average Sales for that month

For example, January's seasonal index is calculated by first finding its monthly average sales, which is (15,200 + 16,100) ÷ 2 = 15,650, and then dividing this value by the overall average of all months (18,921), giving a seasonal index of 15,650 ÷ 18,921 ≈ 0.82. This shows that January typically performs below the average month.

Table 4.14: Monthly sales trends with seasonal adjustment indicators

Month	Year 1 Sales	Year 2 Sales	Monthly Average	Seasonal Index
Jan	15200	16100	15650	0.82
Feb	16800	17900	17350	0.91
...	...	...	...	...
Dec	22100	23400	22750	1.19

This helps adjust forecasts to reflect recurring seasonal patterns.

4.12.1.4 Step 4: Trend-Adjusted Forecast

To create a realistic forecast, we first need to understand how the business is performing overall and how it changes across time.

We start by looking at total yearly sales. When we add up all monthly sales, Year 1 totals 209,000 units, and Year 2 totals 222,400 units. Since Year 2 is higher, this shows that the business is growing. The difference between the two years is 13,400 units, which represents the total increase in sales. To express this as a growth rate, we divide 13,400 by 209,000, which gives approximately 0.064 or 6.4% growth. This means the business grew by about 6.4% from Year 1 to Year 2.

Next, we combine this growth information with what we already learned earlier about seasonality. From the seasonal index, we know that some months are naturally stronger or weaker than others. For example, months like July and December tend to be higher, while months like January and November are usually lower. We also use the monthly average, which represents a normal expected level of sales for each month based on both years of data.

To create the final forecast, we combine all three ideas: the monthly average, the seasonal pattern, and the overall growth of the business. This is done using the formula:

Trend-Adjusted Forecast = Monthly Average × Seasonal Index × 1.064

This means we first adjust each month based on its normal seasonal behavior, and then increase it slightly to reflect overall business growth.

For example, in January the monthly average is 15,650 and the seasonal index is 0.82. First, we adjust for seasonality by multiplying 15,650 by 0.82, which gives 12,833. Then we apply the growth factor by multiplying 12,833 by 1.064, which results in approximately 13,650 units.

Using this same process for all months produces the following forecast:

Table 4.15: Seasonal adjustment and trend-based sales forecast

Month	Monthly Avg	Seasonal Index	Trend-Adjusted Forecast
Jan	15650	0.82	13650
...	...	...	...
Dec	22750	1.19	28790

This final forecast is more accurate than simpler methods because it combines overall business growth with predictable seasonal patterns, giving a more realistic view of future demand.

4.12.1.5 Step 5: Comparing Forecasting Methods

At this point, you have produced three different forecasts for the same data. Each method answers the same question—"what will sales look like next?"—but in different ways.

To understand which method is most useful, we compare the actual forecast values for each month. (3 month moving averages for year 2 are used)

Forecast Comparison Table (Year 3 Forecasts)

Table 4.16: Sales forecasting using moving average, seasonal index, and trend adjustment

Month	3-Month Moving Average	Seasonal Index	Trend-Adjusted Forecast
Jan	17467	15650	13650
...	...	...	...
Dec	18733	22750	28790

What this comparison is showing

The three methods behave very differently:

The 3-month moving average stays closest to recent performance. It smooths the data, so it does not show strong seasonal highs or lows. That is why values stay in a narrower range (about 17,000–22,000).

The seasonal index model creates a repeating pattern across the year. You can clearly see low-demand months like January (15,650) and November (14,750), and high-demand months like July (22,400) and December (22,750).

The trend-adjusted forecast produces the most extreme values because it combines seasonal patterns with overall business growth. That is why peak months such as July (28,130) and December (28,790) are much higher than the other models.

These differences show that forecasting is not about finding one "correct" answer. Instead, each method answers a different business question:

- Moving average → "What is happening right now?"
- Seasonal model → "What happens every year?"
- Trend-adjusted model → "What happens when growth and seasonality combine?"

In real business decisions, companies often compare all three before choosing a final forecast depending on whether they care more about short-term stability or long-term planning.

4.12.1.6 Step 6: Forecast Accuracy Check

At this stage of the lab, we evaluate how accurate each forecasting method was by comparing the predicted values to the actual sales from Year 2. The purpose of this step is not to create a new forecast, but to measure how close each model came to reality. We do this by taking the actual sales value for each month and subtracting the forecasted value from it. This difference is called the forecast error and it tells us how far off the prediction was from what really happened in the business.

The table below shows the actual Year 2 sales alongside the forecasts produced by the three different methods: the 3-month moving average, the seasonal model, and the trend-adjusted model. It also includes the forecast error for each method so that the differences can be clearly seen.

Table 4.17: Forecast components and error comparison across models

Month	Actual (Y2)	Moving Avg	MA Error	Seasonal Value	Seasonal Error	Trend Value	Trend Error
Jan	16100	17467	-1367	15650	450	13650	2450
...	...	...	...	...	...	...	...

When interpreting this table, it is important to understand that each error value represents how far the forecast was from the real sales number. A value close to zero means the forecast was very accurate, while larger positive or negative values mean the model was less accurate. A positive error means the model underestimated sales, while a negative error means it overestimated sales.

The moving average model produces relatively stable results because it is based on recent historical data and smooths out sudden changes. However, it struggles when there are sharp seasonal increases or decreases, which is why some months show larger errors. The seasonal model performs more consistently because it captures the repeating pattern of high and low months throughout the year. Its errors are more uniform, which suggests that seasonality is a strong feature of this dataset. The trend-adjusted model produces the most extreme values because it combines both growth and seasonality, which leads to larger overestimations in high-demand months and larger deviations when the trend assumption does not match actual behavior.

Overall, this comparison shows that there is no single best forecasting method for all situations. Instead, the most reliable method depends on the structure of the data. In this case, the seasonal model appears to be the most consistent because the business shows strong repeating monthly patterns.

4.12.2 Practice

This dataset represents monthly sales for a retail store over a two-year period. The goal of this practice is to understand how sales change over time, identify seasonal patterns, and use those patterns to create forecasts for future months. You will use Excel to calculate a moving average, build a seasonal index, and create a trend-adjusted forecast for Year 3. All calculations should be completed in Excel, and AI tools may be used only to help interpret results after your work is complete.

Table 4.18: Monthly sales comparison between Year 1 and Year 2

Month	Year 1 Sales	Year 2 Sales
Jan	13,500	14,200
Feb	14,900	15,700
Mar	16,200	17,000
Apr	15,300	16,000
May	17,000	18,000
Jun	18,200	19,300
Jul	19,600	20,700
Aug	18,900	20,100
Sep	16,700	17,800
Oct	14,900	15,900
Nov	12,800	13,700
Dec	19,900	21,100

4.12.2.1 Questions

1. Enter the sales data into Excel and reorganize it into one continuous list of 24 months from January Year 1 through December Year 2. Why is it important to arrange the data as a continuous time series?
2. Calculate a 3-month moving average using the monthly sales data. How does the moving average help smooth out changes in sales over time?
3. Calculate the average sales for each month across both years. Use these averages to create a seasonal index for each month. What do the seasonal index values tell

you about sales patterns during different months?

4. Calculate the growth rate between Year 1 and Year 2 sales. Use the growth rate and seasonal index to create a trend-adjusted forecast for Year 3. How does adding growth and seasonality improve the forecast?

5. Compare the results of the 3-month moving average, the seasonal index model, and the trend-adjusted forecast. How are the forecasts different from each other? What does each method show about the business?

6. Compare each forecast to the actual Year 2 sales by calculating forecast errors. Which forecasting method appears to be the most accurate? Why do you think it performed better than the others?

Chapter 5

Predictive Modeling

5.1 Learning Outcomes

5-1. Recognize how businesses use simple relationships between data to make predictions

5-2. Understand basic methods for predicting yes/no business decisions

5-3. Identify how businesses check if their predictions are accurate

5-4. Recognize how computers help businesses make better predictions and explain their reasoning

5.2 Introduction

Imagine you work for a small online bookstore, and your boss asks you an important

question: "Which of our 5,000 customers are most likely to buy something from us next month?" This might seem like an impossible question to answer, but businesses do this kind of prediction every day using something called predictive modeling.

Predictive modeling is like being a fortune teller for businesses, except instead of using crystal balls, you use data and patterns from the past to make educated guesses about the future. It's like how you might predict that your favorite coffee shop will be busy on Monday morning because it's always busy on Monday mornings, or how you know to bring an umbrella when dark clouds are forming.

Think about Netflix recommending movies you might like, or Amazon suggesting products you might want to buy. These companies aren't just guessing - they're using predictive modeling to analyze what you've watched or bought before, compare it to what similar customers have done, and predict what you're likely to enjoy next.

The difference between forecasting (which we learned about in Module 4) and predictive modeling is like the difference between predicting the weather and predicting whether you'll need an umbrella. Forecasting usually looks at how things change over time - like predicting that ice cream sales will be higher in summer. Predictive modeling looks at relationships between different things - like predicting that customers who buy mystery novels are also likely to buy detective shows.

For businesses, good predictions can be incredibly valuable. A clothing store that can predict which customers are likely to buy winter coats can send those customers special offers, while avoiding wasting money on customers who probably won't be interested. A bank that can predict which loan applicants are likely to pay back their loans can make better lending decisions and avoid losing money.

Modern technology has made predictive modeling much more powerful and accessible. Computer programs can now look at huge amounts of information and spot patterns that humans would never notice. However, the basic idea remains the same: look for patterns in what happened before and use those patterns to make smart guesses about what will happen next.

In this module, we'll explore how businesses use predictive modeling to make better decisions. We'll learn to recognize simple relationships between different pieces of business information, understand basic methods for predicting yes/no decisions, see how businesses check whether their predictions are working, and discover how computers help make predictions while explaining their reasoning in ways people can understand.

Whether you're helping a small business decide which customers to contact with special offers or working for a large company trying to predict which products will be popular next season, understanding predictive modeling will help you contribute to smarter business decisions based on data rather than just guesswork.

The goal isn't to become a technical expert who builds complex prediction systems, but to understand how these systems work so you can use them effectively and interpret their results in ways that help businesses succeed.

5.3 Simple Relationships Between Business Data

5.3.1 Understanding How One Thing Affects Another

The simplest form of predictive modeling is looking at how one thing affects another thing in business. This is called simple linear regression, but you can think of it as finding the connection between two pieces of information. It's like discovering that when the temperature goes up, ice cream sales go up too, or when gas prices increase, people drive less.

Businesses use these simple relationships all the time to make predictions and plan. A restaurant might notice that when they spend more money on advertising, they get more customers. A retail store might discover that when they hire more sales staff, their daily sales increase. These relationships help businesses understand what drives their success and make better decisions about where to spend their time and money.

Let's look at a simple example. Imagine a small pizza delivery business that wants to understand the relationship between how much they spend on online advertising each month and how many new customers they get. After looking at six months of data, they might discover a clear pattern: for every extra $100 they spend on advertising, they typically get about 15 new customers.

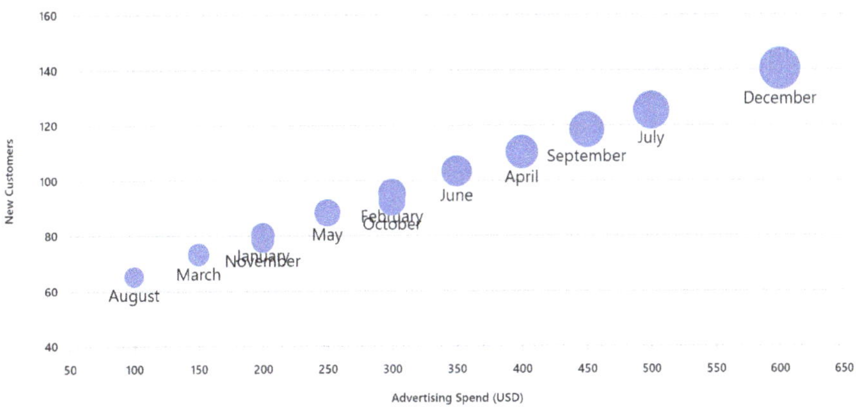

This relationship can be expressed as a simple equation: New Customers = 50 + (0.15 × Advertising Dollars). This means that even with no advertising, they get about 50 new customers per month from word-of-mouth and repeat business. But for every dollar they spend on advertising, they can expect to get 0.15 additional new customers.

Understanding this relationship helps the pizza business make smart decisions. If they want to get 100 new customers next month, they can calculate that they need to spend about $333 on advertising. If their budget only allows $200 for advertising, they can predict they'll get about 80 new customers. This kind of prediction helps with planning staffing, ordering ingredients, and setting realistic sales goals.

However, it's important to understand that these relationships aren't perfect. Real business situations are messier than simple equations. The pizza business might spend $300 on advertising one month and get fewer new customers instead of the predicted. Maybe there was a big snowstorm that kept people home, or maybe a competitor opened nearby. The prediction gives them a good starting point, but they need to be prepared for some variation.

5.3.2 Looking at Multiple Factors at Once

Real business situations usually involve more than just two factors. A pizza business's success doesn't just depend on advertising - it also depends on things like the weather, local events, the quality of their food, their prices, and what their competitors are doing. Multiple regression helps businesses understand how several factors work together to influence outcomes.

Think of it like baking a cake. The result doesn't just depend on how much flour you use - it also depends on the amount of sugar, eggs, butter, and baking time. Each ingredient contributes to the outcome and understanding how they work together helps you bake better cakes. Multiple regression works the same way for business decisions.

Let's expand our pizza business example. After collecting more data, the business might discover that their monthly sales depend on several factors:

- Advertising spending (more advertising = more sales)
- Average temperature (warmer weather = more delivery orders)
- Number of local events (concerts, sports games = more orders)
- Competitor promotions (competitor discounts = fewer sales for them)

A multiple regression analysis might show that their monthly sales can be predicted using this relationship: Monthly Sales = $8,000 + (12 ×$ Advertising Dollars) + $(50 \times AverageTemperature) + (200 ×$ Number of Events) - ($300 × Competitor Promotions).

This more complex relationship gives the business much better predictions because it considers multiple factors that affect their success. They can now predict that if they spend $500 on advertising during a month with an average temperature of 75 degrees, 3 local events, and 2 competitor promotions, their sales will be approximately: $8,000 + (12 × 500) + (50 \times 75) + (200 × 3)$ - ($300 × 2) = $8,000 + $6,000 + $3,750 + $600 - $600 = $17,750.

Understanding these multiple relationships helps businesses make more informed decisions. The pizza business might decide to increase their advertising spending during warm months when the effect will be stronger, or they might plan special promotions to counter competitor activities.

5.3.3 Real Business Example: Predicting Customer Satisfaction

Let's look at how a customer service organization might use simple predictive modeling to improve their operations. The company wants to understand what factors influence customer satisfaction scores, which they measure on a scale from 1 to 10.

After analyzing their data, they discover several important relationships:

Response Time Impact: For every additional hour it takes to respond to a customer inquiry, satisfaction scores drop by an average of 0.3 points. This means that responding in 2 hours instead of 6 hours could improve satisfaction by about 1.2 points.

Agent Experience Impact: Customers served by agents with more than 2 years of experience rate their satisfaction 0.8 points higher on average than customers served by newer agents.

Issue Complexity Impact: Simple issues (like password resets) typically receive satisfaction scores that are 1.5 points higher than complex issues (like technical troubleshooting).

Here's what this data might look like:

Customer	Response Time (hours)	Agent Experience	Issue Type	Satisfaction Score
1	2.0	Experienced	Simple	8.5
2	6.0	New	Complex	5.2
3	1.0	Experienced	Simple	9.1
4	4.0	New	Simple	7.3
5	3.0	Experienced	Complex	6.8
6	8.0	New	Complex	4.1

Using these relationships, the company can predict satisfaction scores for future customers and make operational improvements. They might decide to:

- Set a goal of responding to all inquiries within 3 hours
- Assign complex issues to experienced agents when possible
- Provide additional training to new agents
- Create better tools and procedures for handling complex issues

The predictive model helps them understand not just what happened in the past, but what they can expect in the future if they make specific changes to their operations.

5.3.4 Understanding When Relationships Change

Sometimes the relationship between two business factors isn't the same in all situations. This is called an interaction effect, and it's like discovering that the effect of one thing depends on something else. For example, a retail store might find that having a sale increases customers more during slow periods than during busy periods.

Let's say a coffee shop discovers that playing background music increases customer satisfaction, but the effect depends on the time of day. During quiet morning hours, soft jazz music increases satisfaction scores by 1.2 points. But during busy lunch hours, the same music only increases satisfaction by 0.3 points because customers are more focused on getting their orders quickly.

Understanding these interaction effects helps businesses make more nuanced decisions. The coffee shop might choose to play music during slower periods but focus on faster service during busy times. A clothing store might find that personal attention from sales staff is more valuable for expensive items than for basic items, so they train their staff to spend more time with customers buying higher-priced merchandise.

These kinds of insights show why simple rules like "more advertising always means more sales" aren't always true. The effectiveness of business strategies often depends on the context and other factors happening at the same time.

5.3.5 Making Predictions vs. Understanding Causes

It's important to understand the difference between using data to make predictions and using data to understand what causes what. Predictive modeling is primarily about making good guesses about the future, not necessarily about proving that one thing causes another.

For example, a bookstore might notice that customers who buy coffee also tend to buy more books. They could use this relationship to predict that customers entering the coffee area are likely to make book purchases. However, this doesn't necessarily mean that drinking coffee causes people to buy books. Maybe people who have time to drink coffee also have time to browse books, or maybe book lovers just happen to also be coffee lovers.

For business purposes, this distinction often doesn't matter. If the bookstore can predict that coffee customers will buy more books, they can use this information to make better business decisions - like placing book displays near the coffee area or offering coffee discounts to book buyers. The prediction is valuable even if they don't fully understand the underlying cause.

However, understanding this limitation helps businesses avoid making mistakes. If the bookstore assumes that coffee causes book buying, they might think that giving away free coffee will increase book sales. But if the real relationship is that people with more leisure time tend to buy both coffee and books, free coffee might not have the expected effect.

Good predictive modeling focuses on finding reliable patterns that help make better business decisions, while being honest about what those patterns can and cannot tell us about cause-and-effect relationships.

5.4 Predicting Yes/No Business Decisions

5.4.1 Understanding Classification Problems

Many important business decisions come down to yes or no questions. Will a customer buy our product? Should we approve this loan application? Is this email spam? Will this employee stay with the company for another year? These types of predictions are called classification problems because they involve putting things into categories rather than predicting specific numbers.

Classification is different from the regression we learned about in the previous section. Regression predicts numbers - like how much a customer will spend or what a house will sell for. Classification predicts categories - like whether a customer will respond to an email campaign (yes or no) or which of several customer types a person belongs to (budget-conscious, premium, or luxury shopper).

Think about how a bank decides whether to approve a credit card application. They can't predict exactly how much money an applicant will spend or whether they'll pay back every penny. But they can predict whether the applicant falls into the "likely to be a good customer" category or the "likely to cause problems" category. This yes/no decision is much more practical for the bank's purposes.

The consequences of getting classification predictions wrong are often different from regression errors. If a store predicts a customer will spend \$100 but they spend \$90, that's a \$10 error. But if a bank predicts a loan applicant is low risk when they're high-risk, the bank might lose thousands of dollars. Classification errors are often more about being completely right or completely wrong rather than being close to the right answer.

Let's look at how an online retailer might approach the classification problem of predicting which customers will respond to an email promotion. Instead of trying to predict exactly how much each customer will spend (which would be regression), they focus on the simpler question: will this customer make any purchase after receiving the email?

5.4.2 Logistic Regression: Predicting Probabilities

Logistic regression is a method that helps businesses predict the probability that something will fall into a particular category. Instead of just saying "yes" or "no," it gives you a percentage chance, like "this customer has a 75% chance of responding to our email campaign."

Think of logistic regression like a more sophisticated version of the simple relationships we learned about earlier but designed specifically for yes/no questions. Instead of predicting a specific number, it predicts the likelihood that something will happen.

Let's say an online clothing store wants to predict which customers are likely to make a purchase in the next month. They might look at factors like:

- How recently the customer made their last purchase
- How much they typically spend per order
- How many emails they've opened in the past month
- Whether they've browsed the website recently

The logistic regression analysis might reveal patterns like:

- Customers who made a purchase in the last 30 days have a 65% chance of buying again next month
- Customers who haven't purchased in 90+ days only have a 15% chance of buying next month
- Customers who open emails regularly are 2.3 times more likely to make a purchase than those who don't

Here's what this might look like in a simple data table:

Customer	Days Since Last Purchase	Email Opens (Last Month)	Average Order Value	Purchase Probability
A	15	8	75	78%
B	120	0	45	12%
C	45	3	120	45%
D	8	12	200	85%
E	200	1	30	8%

This probability information is incredibly valuable for business decisions. The clothing store might decide to:

- Send special offers to customers with 40-70% purchase probability to push them over the edge
- Focus retention efforts on high-value customers whose probability is dropping
- Avoid spending marketing money on customers with very low probability

The beauty of probability predictions is that they help businesses make more nuanced decisions than simple yes/no classifications. A customer with 60% purchase probability might get a different marketing approach than a customer with 20% probability.

5.4.3 Decision Trees: Following Business Logic

Decision trees provide another approach to classification that works more like human decision-making. Instead of using mathematical formulas, decision trees create a series of simple yes/no questions that lead to a final decision. They're called trees because they branch out like a tree, with each branch representing a different path to a decision.

Think about how a manager might decide whether to approve a customer's request for a refund. They might follow a mental process like: "Is the item returnable? If yes, was it returned within 30 days? If yes, is the item in good condition? If yes, approve the refund." Decision trees work the same way, but they use data to figure out the best questions to ask and in what order.

Let's look at how a small business might use a decision tree to decide which customers to call with a special offer. Based on their experience, they might create a decision tree like this:

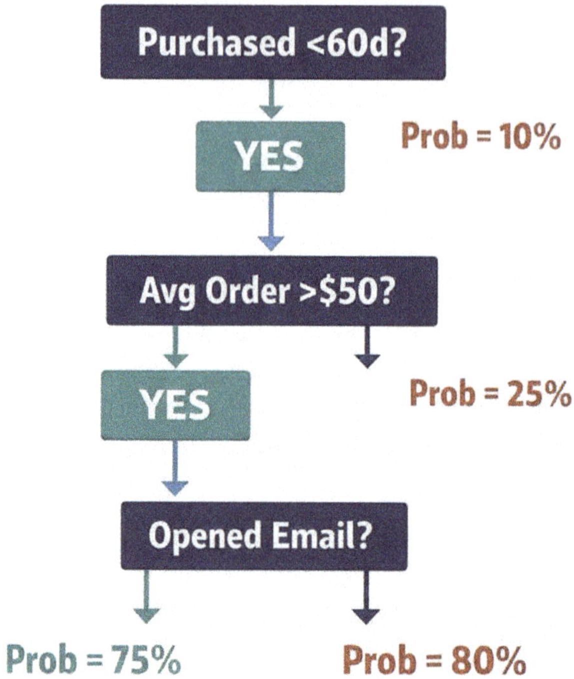

Step 1:

Has the customer purchased in the last 60 days?

- If YES, go to Step 2
- If NO, probability of purchase = 10% (probably not worth calling)

Step 2: Is the customer's average order value above $50?

- If YES, go to Step 3
- If NO, probability of purchase = 25% (maybe worth calling during slow periods)

Step 3: Has the customer opened our emails in the last month?

- If YES, probability of purchase = 75% (definitely worth calling)
- If NO, probability of purchase = 40% (worth calling if we have time)

This decision tree gives the business a clear, logical process for deciding which customers to contact. It's easy to understand, easy to explain to employees, and easy to follow consistently.

Here's how this might work with actual customer data:

Customer	Last Purchase (Days Ago)	Avg Order Value	Opened Emails	Recent Decision Path	Call Priority
Smith	25	85	Yes	Step 1→2→3	High (75%)
Jones	45	35	No	Step 1→2	Medium (25%)
Brown	90	120	Yes	Step 1	Low (10%)
Davis	30	65	No	Step 1→2→3	Medium (40%)

Decision trees are particularly valuable because they're easy to understand and explain. A sales manager can easily train new employees to follow the decision tree, and customers can understand the logic if they ask why they received or didn't receive a call.

5.4.4 Combining Multiple Approaches

Many businesses achieve better results by combining classification methods rather than relying on a single approach. This is similar to getting a second opinion from a doctor—different methods can detect different patterns, and integrating their insights often leads to more accurate decisions.

For example, a subscription service predicting which customers might cancel could use logistic regression to score customers based on cancellation risk, decision trees to identify reasons for high-risk cancellations, and simple business rules (e.g., customers who call support more than three times a month are high risk) to catch edge cases.

By combining these approaches, logistic regression might identify 80% of potential cancellations, decision trees could clarify why customers cancel, and simple rules catch unusual cases the others miss. A practical workflow could involve scoring all customers with logistic regression, categorizing high-risk customers using decision trees, and applying retention strategies tailored to the predicted reasons for cancellation.

5.4.5 Real Business Example: Email Marketing Classification

A small e-commerce business can use classification to improve its email marketing by predicting which customers are likely to make a purchase after receiving a promotional email. By analyzing customer, email, and behavioral factors—such as time since last purchase, total past purchases, average order value, day and time of email sent, subject line type, email open rate, recent website visits, and items left in the cart—the company can estimate each customer's likelihood of responding.

Using this information, the business can segment customers and tailor its approach: high-value recent customers (25% response probability) receive all promotional emails, regular customers (12%) get targeted emails, occasional customers (6%) are sent only major sales and announcements, and inactive customers (2%) receive re-engagement campaigns or are removed from the list.

This system improves email deliverability, increases revenue by focusing on responsive customers, reduces costs by avoiding wasted emails, and enhances customer satisfaction through more relevant messaging. The key takeaway is that recognizing differences in customer behavior and adjusting communication accordingly leads to better business outcomes than a one-size-fits-all approach.

5.5 Checking If Predictions Are Working

5.5.1 Understanding Prediction Accuracy

Just like you'd want to know if a weather forecast is usually right before deciding whether to bring an umbrella, businesses need to know how accurate their predictions are before making important decisions based on them. Checking prediction accuracy is like giving your prediction system a report card to see how well it's performing.

The challenge is that different types of prediction problems need different ways of measuring success. If you're predicting how much money customers will spend, being off by $5 might be fine, but being off by $500 is a big problem. If you're predicting whether customers will respond to an email campaign, you either get it right or wrong - there's no ”close enough.”

For yes/no predictions (like whether a customer will buy something), accuracy is often measured as the percentage of predictions that turn out to be correct. If a business predicts that 100 customers will respond to an email campaign, and 85 of them actually do respond, that's 85% accuracy. This seems straightforward, but it can be misleading in some situations.

Imagine a business where only 5% of customers typically respond to email campaigns. A prediction system that always says ”no, this customer won't respond” would be right 95% of the time, but it would be completely useless for business purposes because it would never identify the customers who actually will respond.

This is why businesses often look at more detailed measures of accuracy that consider different types of mistakes separately. Getting a ”yes” prediction wrong is different from getting a ”no” prediction wrong, and the business impact of these different mistakes can be very different.

5.5.2 Different Types of Prediction Mistakes

When businesses make yes/no predictions, there are four possible outcomes which can be tabled in a confusion matrix, and understanding each one helps evaluate how well the prediction system is working.

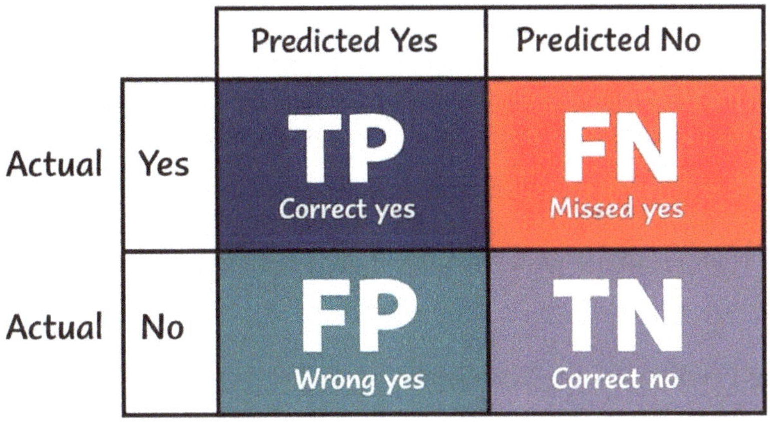

True Positives: The prediction says "yes" and it's correct. For example, predicting that a customer will respond to an email campaign, and they do respond. These are the predictions that directly help the business succeed.

True Negatives: The prediction says "no" and it's correct. For example, predicting that a customer won't respond to an email campaign, and they don't respond. These predictions help the business avoid wasting resources.

False Positives: The prediction says "yes" but it's wrong. For example, predicting that a customer will respond to an email campaign, but they don't respond. These mistakes can waste marketing budget and resources.

False Negatives: The prediction says "no" but it's wrong. For example, predicting that a customer won't respond to an email campaign, but they would have responded. These mistakes represent missed opportunities.

Let's look at how this works with a concrete example. A small online store sends promotional emails to 1,000 customers and uses a prediction system to decide which customers are likely to make a purchase:

Prediction Result	Number of Customers	Business Impact
True Positives	80	Successfully identified responsive customers
True Negatives	850	Correctly avoided wasting emails on unresponsive customers
False Positives	50	Wasted email sends to unresponsive customers
False Negatives	20	Missed opportunities with responsive customers

The overall accuracy is 93% (930 correct predictions out of 1,000), which sounds great.

But looking at the details reveals more nuanced insights:

- **Precision**: Of the 130 customers predicted to respond, 80 did (80/130 = 62%). This measures how often "yes" predictions are correct.
- **Recall**: Of the 100 customers who responded, 80 were correctly identified (80/100 = 80%). This measures how many responsive customers were found.

Understanding these different measures helps businesses make better decisions about their prediction systems. High precision means less wasted effort on customers who won't respond. High recall means fewer missed opportunities with customers who would respond.

5.5.3 Testing Predictions on New Data

The most important test of any prediction system is how well it works on new data that it hasn't seen before. A prediction system might appear very accurate when tested on the same data used to create it but perform poorly when applied to new situations. This is like a student who memorizes specific test questions but can't apply the concepts to new problems.

To avoid this problem, businesses typically split their historical data into two parts: a training set used to build the prediction system, and a test set used to evaluate how well it works. The test set simulates what would happen when the prediction system encounters new customers or situations.

Let's say a subscription service wants to predict which customers might cancel their subscriptions. They have data on 10,000 customers from the past year. They might use this approach:

Training Data (8,000 customers): Used to build the prediction system by finding patterns between customer characteristics and cancellation behavior.

Test Data (2,000 customers): Used to evaluate the prediction system by seeing how accurately it predicts cancellations for customers it hasn't seen before.

If the prediction system achieves 85% accuracy on the training data but only 70% accuracy on the test data, this suggests the system might be "overfitted" - too specifically tuned to the training data to work well in new situations.

Cross-validation provides an even more thorough approach to testing. Instead of splitting data once, cross-validation splits the data multiple times and tests the prediction system on each split. This gives a more reliable estimate of how the system will perform on new data.

For example, 5-fold cross-validation would:

1. Split the 10,000 customers into 5 groups of 2,000 each
2. Train the prediction system on 4 groups and test on the remaining group
3. Repeat this process 5 times, using each group as the test set once

4. Average the results to get a robust estimate of prediction accuracy

This approach helps businesses understand not just how accurate their predictions are on average, but also how much the accuracy varies in different situations.

5.5.4 Real Business Example: Customer Service Prediction Accuracy

Let's examine how a customer service organization might evaluate their system for predicting which support tickets will require escalation to senior staff. This is important because escalated tickets are expensive to handle, but customers get frustrated if their complex issues aren't escalated when they should be.

The company analyzes 5,000 support tickets from the past six months and builds a prediction system based on factors like:

- Type of issue reported
- Customer's account status and history
- Time of day the ticket was submitted
- Initial customer satisfaction rating

Here's how their prediction system performs:

Actual Outcome	Predicted: Escalate	Predicted: Don't Escalate	Total
Actually Escalated	180	45	225
Not Escalated	120	4655	4775
Total	300	4700	5000

From this confusion matrix, the company can calculate several important metrics:

Overall Accuracy: (180 + 4,655) / 5,000 = 96.7% This looks very good, but let's dig deeper.

Precision: 180 / 300 = 60% When the system predicts escalation is needed, it's correct 60% of the time. This means 40% of escalations are unnecessary, which wastes senior staff time.

Recall: 180 / 225 = 80% The system correctly identifies 80% of tickets that need escalation. This means 20% of complex issues aren't escalated when they should be potentially frustrating customers.

Cost Analysis:

- 120 unnecessary escalations × \$50 per escalation = \$6,000 in wasted costs
- 45 missed escalations × \$200 per customer complaint = \$9,000 in customer service costs

This analysis helps the company understand that while their prediction system has high overall accuracy, the business impact of different types of mistakes varies significantly.

Missing an escalation (false negative) cost twice as much as an unnecessary escalation (false positive).

Based on this analysis, the company might decide to adjust their prediction system to be more sensitive, accepting more unnecessary escalations to catch more of the tickets that truly need escalation. This would improve customer satisfaction at the cost of some additional staff time.

5.5.5 Monitoring Predictions Over Time

Prediction systems don't stay accurate forever. Business conditions change, customer behavior evolves, and relationships that were true in the past might not hold in the future. This is why businesses need to continuously monitor their prediction accuracy and update their systems when performance starts to decline.

Think about how a retail store's customer behavior might change during different seasons, economic conditions, or in response to new competitors. A prediction system that works well during normal times might become less accurate during a recession, holiday season, or when a major competitor opens nearby.

Regular monitoring might involve:

- **Weekly accuracy checks**: Quick reviews of how well predictions matched actual outcomes
- **Monthly detailed analysis**: Deeper investigation of which types of predictions are becoming less accurate
- **Quarterly system updates**: Retraining prediction systems with new data to maintain accuracy

For example, an e-commerce company might notice that their customer purchase predictions become less accurate during holiday seasons because customer behavior changes significantly. They might develop separate prediction systems for different times of year or adjust their existing system to account for seasonal factors.

The key is recognizing that prediction systems require ongoing maintenance and improvement, just like any other business tool. Regular monitoring helps ensure that businesses continue to make good decisions based on accurate predictions rather than relying on outdated models that no longer reflect current reality.

5.6 How Computers Help Make Better Predictions

5.6.1 The Rise of Smart Prediction Systems

Modern computers have revolutionized how businesses make predictions by automating many tasks that used to require specialized expertise and taking much longer to complete. Today's prediction software can automatically analyze large amounts of data, test different prediction methods, and even explain why it made specific predictions - all without requiring users to be technical experts.

Think about the difference between doing math by hand versus using a calculator. The calculator doesn't just make calculations faster - it also reduces errors and allows you to solve more complex problems. Smart prediction systems work the same way for business forecasting. They can consider many more factors, test many more possibilities, and find patterns that humans might miss.

Traditional prediction methods required people to manually examine data, decide which factors might be important, choose appropriate analysis techniques, and interpret the results. This process was time-consuming, required specialized training, and often produced different results depending on who was doing the analysis. Modern AI-powered systems can automate much of this work while producing more consistent and often more accurate results.

For example, a small retail business trying to predict which products will be popular next month used to require hiring a data analyst who would spend days or weeks examining sales data, seasonal patterns, and market trends. Today, the same business can use automated prediction software that analyzes all this information in minutes and provides clear recommendations about inventory planning.

However, it's important to understand that these smart systems don't replace human judgment - they enhance it. The most successful businesses combine computer-powered analysis with human understanding of their customers, markets, and business goals. Computers excel at finding patterns in data, while humans excel at understanding what those patterns mean for business strategy.

5.6.2 Machine Learning: Systems That Learn from Experience

Machine learning represents a major advance in prediction technology because these systems can improve their performance over time by learning from new data. Instead of following pre-programmed rules, machine learning systems discover patterns on their own and adjust their predictions based on what they learn.

Think of machine learning like teaching a computer to recognize patterns the same way you might teach a child to recognize different types of dogs. You show the child many examples of different dogs, pointing out features that distinguish breeds. Eventually, the child learns to identify breeds on their own, even for dogs they've never seen before. Machine learning works similarly - you show the computer lots of examples of business data and outcomes, and it learns to identify patterns that predict future results.

A practical example is an online store using machine learning to predict which customers are likely to return purchased items. The system analyzes thousands of past orders, considering factors such as product categories and prices, customer purchase history and demographics, seasonal patterns and timing, product reviews and ratings, and shipping and delivery information. Over time, the system may identify patterns, such as customers buying clothing items in December for holiday gifts being 40% more likely to return items, first-time customers being twice as likely to return items as repeat customers, products with average ratings below 4.0 stars having 60% higher return rates, and customers who read reviews before purchasing being 30% less likely to return items. The strength of machine learning lies in its ability to automatically detect these patterns and continuously update predictions as new data becomes available, adapting to changes in customer behavior or emerging trends.

5.6.3 Ensemble Methods: Combining Multiple Predictions

One of the most effective techniques in modern prediction systems is ensemble modeling, which combines multiple prediction methods to achieve more accurate results than any single approach. It's like gathering several expert opinions before making a decision.

For example, when choosing a restaurant, you might check reviews, ask friends, look at menus, and consider location. Each source gives a different perspective, and combining them leads to a better choice. Ensemble prediction systems work similarly, combining simple statistical methods, machine learning algorithms, business rules, and time-based forecasting to capture a wide range of patterns.

A restaurant chain predicting daily customer traffic might use weather-based predictions, calendar-based trends, long-term trend analysis, and machine learning. Each method may produce slightly different forecasts, but when combined, the ensemble system generates a final prediction that is more reliable than any individual method. For instance, weather predictions might suggest 180 customers, calendar patterns 165, trend analysis 175, and machine learning 172. The ensemble average of 173 customers incorporates all insights, offering higher confidence and accuracy.

5.6.4 Explainable AI: Understanding Why Predictions Are Made

Advanced prediction systems can sometimes act as "black boxes," giving accurate results without explaining how they reached them. This lack of transparency can be a problem for businesses that need to justify decisions, especially in regulated industries or customer-facing operations.

Explainable AI solves this by providing clear, human-understandable reasons behind predictions. For example, instead of just stating that a customer has a 75% chance of responding to an email, an explainable system might detail that the customer opened eight emails last month (+20%), made a recent purchase (+30%), and has a high average order value (+25%).

These explanations help build trust by showing users the logic behind predictions, identify potential problems if inappropriate factors are used, improve decision-making by clarifying actionable insights, and meet regulatory requirements that demand transparency.

In a customer service setting, explainable AI might predict ticket urgency. For instance, a premium customer with a complex technical issue and multiple prior contacts could be flagged as high urgency (85%), while a first-time customer with a routine billing question might be medium urgency (45%), and a basic account customer with a general inquiry could be low urgency (20%). Such explanations guide managers not just in prioritizing tickets, but also in understanding why certain cases need attention and what actions are most appropriate.

5.6.5 Implementing AI Prediction Tools in Small Businesses

Modern AI prediction tools are now accessible to small businesses that previously couldn't afford advanced analytics. Cloud-based services and user-friendly software make it possible for companies without technical expertise to benefit from sophisticated predictions.

However, simply buying AI software isn't enough for success. Businesses need to start with clean, organized data, ensuring that customer information, sales records, and other relevant data are accurate and well-structured. They should also focus on simple, well-defined business problems rather than trying to predict everything at once—for example, deciding which customers to target with special offers or how much inventory to order next month.

The most effective approach combines AI insights with human expertise. AI can identify patterns and generate predictions, but business knowledge is essential for interpreting results and making final decisions. Ongoing monitoring and adjustment are also crucial, as AI systems need attention to remain effective as conditions change. Additionally, employees must be trained to understand and use AI predictions in their decision-making.

For example, a small e-commerce business might implement AI-powered customer segmentation gradually. In the first two months, it would clean up customer data and implement basic tracking. Months three and four could involve using AI to identify customer segments based on purchase behavior. Months five and six might test marketing approaches for each segment, followed by measuring results and refining strategies in months seven and eight. From month nine onward, the system would be continuously monitored and improved.

The key is to start simple, learn from experience, and expand AI use gradually. This approach allows small businesses to leverage advanced prediction capabilities without large technology investments or specialized staff, while ensuring AI enhances—not replaces—human business judgment.

5.7 Conclusion

Predictive analytics empowers businesses to make informed, data-driven decisions by analyzing patterns and forecasting future outcomes. Through classification, ensemble modeling, and machine learning, businesses can predict customer behavior, optimize marketing campaigns, manage inventory, and improve operational efficiency. Explainable AI ensures transparency, allowing managers to understand the reasoning behind predictions, build trust, and make actionable decisions. Across all use cases, the combination of AI insights and human expertise creates more reliable, practical outcomes than relying on either alone.

Implementing predictive analytics effectively requires clean, organized data, clearly defined business objectives, and a phased approach. Small businesses benefit by starting with simple projects, testing strategies, monitoring results, and refining models over time. Training employees to understand AI predictions and incorporating them into daily decision-making ensures that AI complements human judgment. When applied thoughtfully, predictive analytics enables small businesses to compete effectively, enhance customer experiences, and improve efficiency without heavy investments in technology or specialized staff.

5.8 Key Terms

Predictive Analytics – Using historical data and statistical methods to forecast future business outcomes.

AI Prediction Tools – Software or systems that generate predictions based on data patterns.

Classification – Assigning data points to categories based on their attributes or predicted behavior.

Ensemble Modeling – Combining multiple predictive methods to achieve higher accuracy.

Explainable AI (XAI) – AI systems that provide clear, understandable reasons for their predictions.

Customer Segmentation – Dividing customers into groups based on behavior, preferences, or demographics.

Data Quality – The accuracy, completeness, and organization of data used for predictions.

Behavioral Data – Information on customer actions, such as purchases, website visits, or email interactions.

Cloud-Based Services – Online platforms providing AI tools without requiring local infrastructure.

Monitoring and Adjustment – Continuously evaluating and updating predictive models to maintain accuracy.

5.9 Review Questions

1. What is predictive analytics, and how can it benefit businesses?
2. How do classification and ensemble modeling differ in predictive analytics?
3. Why is explainable AI important for trust and decision-making?
4. How does customer segmentation improve marketing and service strategies?
5. What makes data "high quality" for predictive analytics purposes?
6. Why should AI predictions be combined with human expertise?
7. How can behavioral data enhance the accuracy of predictions?
8. What advantages do cloud-based AI services provide for small businesses?
9. Why is monitoring and adjusting predictive models essential over time?
10. What are the benefits of implementing predictive analytics gradually rather than all at once?

5.10 References

[1] Hurree. (2024). *Measuring the ROI of AI in Marketing: Key Metrics and Strategies for Marketers*. https://blog.hurree.co/measuring-the-roi-of-ai-in-marketing-key-metrics-and-strategies-for-marketers

[2] SuperAGI. (2024). *Mastering Explainable AI in 2025: A Beginner's Guide to Transparent and Interpretable Models*. https://superagi.com/mastering-explainable-ai-in-2025-a-beginners-guide-to-transparent-and-interpretable-models/

[3] StatusNeo. (2024). *Regression Analysis in Consulting: Unlock Business Insights.* https://statusneo.com/regression-analysis-in-consulting/

[4] Towards Data Science. (2024). *Model Validation Techniques Explained: A Visual Guide with Code Examples.* https://towardsdatascience.com/model-validation-techniques-explained-a-visual-guide-with-code-examples-eb13bbdc8f88/

[5] Fiddler AI. (2024). *Evaluating the ROI of AI Explainability Tools.* https://www.fiddler.ai/articles/evaluating-the-roi-of-ai-explainability-tools

5.11 Lab 5-1 Predictive Modeling

In this lab, you will explore how predictive modeling can be used to make data-driven business decisions using Excel. You will build both single-factor and multi-factor regression models to analyze relationships between variables, generate forecasts, and evaluate model accuracy. In addition, you will learn how to interpret results to support real-world decision-making.

Through this exercise, you will gain practical experience in forecasting outcomes, assessing model performance, and translating data into actionable insights.

5.11.1 Demonstration

A pizza delivery business wants to predict new customers based on advertising spending, temperature, and local events. Management will use predictions to plan budgets and staffing.

Table 5.6: Marketing activity, environmental factors, and customer acquisition by month

Month	Advertising	Avg Temp	Events	New Customers
Jan	200	30	1	78
Feb	250	35	0	82
Mar	300	45	2	88
Apr	350	55	1	96
May	400	65	3	104
Jun	450	75	2	110
Jul	500	80	4	118
Aug	480	78	2	114
Sep	420	70	1	106
Oct	360	60	0	98
Nov	280	50	1	88
Dec	220	35	0	80

5.11.1.1 Step 1: Basic regression

To create a single-factor regression model, first highlight the data in Excel for the Advertising ($) column along with the corresponding values in the New Customers column, making sure no other columns are included. Next, go to the Insert tab and choose a Scatter (X, Y) chart, selecting the option with only markers to display the relationship between the two variables.

Once the chart appears, click on any of the data points, right-click, and select Add Trendline. In the trendline options, choose a Linear trendline and enable Display Equation on Chart so the regression equation is shown directly on the graph.

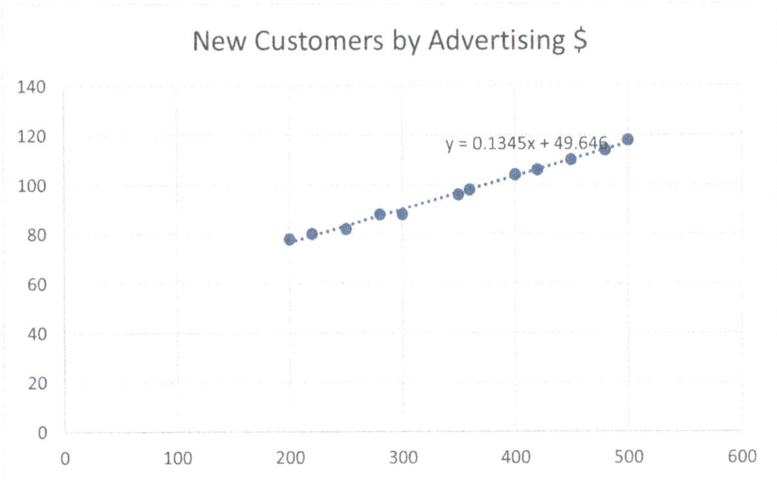

5.11.1.2 Step 2: Predict new customers

This step uses the trendline equation y=0.1423x+47.318 to make predictions about future values. A trendline represents the general relationship between advertising spending (x) and the number of new customers (y) based on the given data. By substituting new advertising amounts into the equation, we can estimate how many customers are expected even for values not directly shown in the data.

For an advertising amount of $550, substituting into the equation gives

y=0.1423(550)+47.318=125.585,

which is approximately 126 customers.

For$600, y=0.1423(600)+47.318=132.815, which is approximately 133 customers.

Therefore, the model predicts about 126 new customers at $550 and about 133 new customers at $600.

5.11.1.3 Step 3: Multi-Factor Regression

In real-world data, outcomes are rarely influenced by a single factor. Instead, several variables often act together to affect a result. A multi-factor regression model is used to capture this relationship by measuring how multiple independent variables jointly influence one dependent variable. In this case, the purpose is to predict New Customers using three factors: Advertising, Average Temperature, and Local Events.

The regression process produces a single mathematical equation that combines all variables into one predictive model. Each independent variable is assigned a coefficient that represents its individual impact on New Customers, while the intercept represents the baseline value when all variables are zero. Together, these values allow us to estimate customer numbers more accurately by accounting for multiple influences at the same time.

This relationship is expressed in the form:

New Customers = a(Advertising) + b(Avg Temp) + c(Local Events) + d

where a, b, and c are the coefficients for each independent variable, and d is the intercept.

Table 5.7: Marketing activity and customer acquisition (partial monthly view)

Month	Advertising	Avg Temp	Events	New Customers
Jan	200	30	1	78
Feb	250	35	0	82

In this dataset, each row represents a month, with Advertising ($), Avg Temp (°F), and Local Events as the independent variables, and New Customers as the dependent variable being predicted.

Once the data is organized in this structure, the regression model can be calculated using Excel's LINEST function. This function allows Excel to determine how each independent variable contributes to changes in the number of new customers.

Select a horizontal range of empty cells (at least four cells in a row to allow space for all outputs). Then enter the formula:

=LINEST(E2:E13, B2:D13, TRUE, TRUE)

Here, E2:E13 represents the range for New Customers, while B2:D13 includes the independent variables Advertising, Avg Temp, and Local Events. The logical value TRUE tells Excel to include the intercept in the model and return full statistical results. When entered in Excel 365, the results automatically spill across the selected cells.

These are the results from the LINEST regression output, which Excel produces when it calculates the multi-factor regression model. Each value has a specific meaning and together they form the final prediction equation.

The first row contains the most important values: the coefficients for each independent variable and the intercept. In this case, the coefficient for Advertising is 0.4556, meaning that for each additional unit of advertising, new customers are expected to increase by about 0.46 (holding other factors constant). The coefficient for Avg Temp is 0.2170, showing a moderate positive relationship with customer numbers. The coefficient for Local Events is 0.0934, meaning each additional event slightly increases expected customers. The final value, 51.1440, is the intercept, which represents the baseline number of customers when all variables are zero.

These values form the regression equation:

"New Customers" = 0.4556("Advertising") + 0.2170("Avg Temp") + 0.0934("Local Events") + 51.1440

The remaining rows in the output provide additional statistical information about the model's accuracy and reliability. These include measures such as standard errors, goodness of fit, and overall variation explained by the model. However, for prediction purposes, the first row (coefficients and intercept) is the most important.

5.11.1.4 Step 4: Make a multivariate prediction

This prediction is a "what-if" analysis, where the regression equation is used to estimate the number of new customers under specific conditions. Instead of relying on past observed months, we substitute hypothetical values into the model to see what the outcome would be if Advertising = 500, Average Temperature = 77°F, and Local Events = 3. This allows us to test how the system is expected to behave under a given set of inputs.

Using the regression equation:

"New Customers" = 0.4556("Advertising") + 0.2170("Avg Temp") + 0.0934("Local Events") + 51.1440

Substitute the values:

$= 0.4556(500) + 0.2170(77) + 0.0934(3) + 51.1440$

Now calculate each part:

$0.4556 \times 500 = 227.8$

$0.2170 \times 77 = 16.709$

$0.0934 \times 3 = 0.2802$

Intercept = 51.1440

Add them together:

$227.8 + 16.709 + 0.2802 + 51.1440 = 295.9332$

So, the predicted number of new customers is approximately 296 customers.

5.11.1.5 Step 5: Evaluating Model Accuracy

After building the regression model, the first step in evaluating accuracy is to generate predicted values for each month using the regression equation. In Excel, this is done by creating a new column called Predicted Customers and applying the model directly to each row of data. Each prediction is calculated using the coefficients from the regression output, multiplying them by their corresponding variables in that row.

For example, in Excel the formula is entered in the first row of the new column as:

=0.4556*B2 + 0.2170*C2 + 0.0934*D2 + 51.1440

This formula uses Advertising, Avg Temp, and Local Events from that row and applies the regression equation to produce a predicted number of customers. Once entered, the formula is copied down so that every month has a predicted value generated by the model.

After predictions are created, the model is evaluated by comparing them to the actual values in the dataset. This is done by calculating the residual, which measures the difference between observed and predicted values:

=E2 - F2

Here, column E contains the actual number of new customers, and column F contains the predicted values. The residual shows how far off the model is for each month, where positive values indicate underprediction and negative values indicate overprediction.

Because positive and negative errors can cancel each other out, the next step is to convert all errors into positive values using the absolute error:

=ABS(G2)

This ensures that only the size of the error is measured, not the direction.

Finally, the overall accuracy of the model is summarized using the Mean Absolute Error (MAE):

=AVERAGE(H2:H13)

This value represents the average size of the model's prediction error across all months. A lower MAE indicates that the regression model closely matches the actual data, while a higher MAE indicates weaker predictive performance.

Table 5.8: Advertising model predictions and error metrics

Month	Advertising	Avg Temp	Events	New Customers	Predicted Customers	Residual	Abs Error
Jan	200	30	1	78	148.9	-70.9	70.9
Feb	250	35	0	82	172.6	-90.6	90.6
...	...	...	...	...	...	...	...
	Mean Abs Error						126.5

The regression model was evaluated by comparing predicted values against the actual number of new customers across all months. After applying the regression equation in Excel, a predicted value was generated for each observation based on Advertising, Average Temperature, and Local Events. These predictions were then directly compared to the actual values to assess model performance.

The results show a consistent pattern of systematic overprediction, where predicted values are significantly higher than the observed customer counts in every month. This is confirmed by the residuals, which are all negative, meaning the model consistently estimates more customers than actually occurred. This indicates that while the model captures directionality between variables, it does not accurately capture the true scale of the relationship in the dataset.

To quantify overall error, the absolute values of the residuals were averaged to compute the Mean Absolute Error (MAE), which is approximately 126.5. This means that, on average, the model's predictions deviate from actual customer values by about 126 customers per month, which is large relative to the observed range of 78 to 118 customers.

Overall, while the regression equation is mathematically correct, the evaluation shows that the model has poor predictive accuracy for this dataset, as evidenced by consistently large residuals and a high MAE. This suggests that the model is not well-calibrated to the scale of the data and would require re-specification or transformation of variables to produce reliable forecasts.

5.11.2 Practice

A customer service department wants to predict satisfaction scores (1–10) based on Response Time (hrs), Agent Experience, and Issue Complexity.

Table 5.9: Customer support response metrics and satisfaction scores

Customer	Response Time (hrs)	Agent Experience	Issue Type	Satisfaction Score
1	2.0	Experienced	Simple	8.5
2	6.0	New	Complex	5.2
3	1.0	Experienced	Simple	9.1
...	...	...	...	...
24	3.0	Experienced	Simple	8.6

5.11.2.1 Questions

1. Convert the categorical variables in the dataset so they can be used in a regression model (Agent Experience and Issue Type).
2. Identify which column represents the dependent variable and which columns represent the independent variables.
3. Create a scatter plot in Excel showing the relationship between Response Time and Satisfaction Score.
4. Add a linear trendline to your scatter plot and display the equation on the chart.
5. Use the trendline equation to estimate Satisfaction Scores for Response Time values of 3.0 hours and 6.0 hours.
6. Run a multiple regression using Response Time, Agent Experience, and Issue Type as predictor variables for Satisfaction Score.
7. Record the regression equation by listing the intercept and all coefficients from your output.
8. Use the regression equation to calculate predicted Satisfaction Scores for all 24 customers.
9. Compute the residuals by subtracting predicted values from actual values, and then calculate absolute errors.
10. Calculate the Mean Absolute Error (MAE) and interpret whether the model performance is strong, moderate, or weak.

5.12 Lab 5-2 Classification

This lab introduces classification modeling, where the goal is to predict categories rather than numeric values. Instead of forecasting quantities, classification helps answer business questions such as yes or no, will respond or will not respond, or approved versus rejected. These models are widely used in marketing, customer targeting, fraud detection, and decision automation.

In this lab, you will use Excel to build a simple classification model using logistic regression concepts, apply decision thresholds to convert probabilities into final predictions, and evaluate model performance using standard classification metrics such as accuracy, precision, and recall. The focus is on understanding how data-driven probability outputs can be transformed into practical business decisions.

5.12.1 Demonstration

A small online retailer wants to predict which customers will respond to a promotional email. Management will use these predictions to prioritize marketing efforts and maximize revenue.

Table 5.10: Customer engagement and response behavior dataset

Customer	Days Since Last Purchase	Email Opens (Last Month)	Avg Order Value ($)	Responded?
A	15	8	75	Yes
B	120	0	45	No
C	45	3	120	No
D	8	12	200	Yes
E	200	1	30	No
F	30	5	80	Yes
G	60	2	50	No
H	10	9	150	Yes
I	150	0	40	No
J	20	7	90	Yes
K	90	1	55	No
L	25	6	85	Yes

5.12.1.1 Step 1: Encode data

The first step is to prepare the dataset so Excel can process it numerically. The outcome variable, Responded?, is originally categorical (Yes/No), but regression-based models require numerical inputs. To solve this, convert the values so that Yes = 1 and No = 0. This allows Excel to interpret response behaviour as a measurable variable rather than text.

To make Excel do this automatically, you convert the text values using a simple formula in a new column.

In Excel, next to the Responded? column, enter:

=IF(E2=”Yes”,1,0)

Then copy this formula down for all rows in the dataset.

This tells Excel: if the response is "Yes", assign a value of 1; if it is anything else (No), assign a value of 0. Once filled down, Excel has a fully numeric version of the outcome variable, which can now be used in regression and probability-based modelling.

Once completed, the dataset now contains one binary dependent variable and three independent variables: Days Since Last Purchase, Email Opens, and Average Order Value.

5.12.1.2 Step 2: Build a simple prediction score

Classification models work by turning input data into a score that reflects how strongly each case belongs to the "Yes" class. In a full analytics tool, this score might come from logistic regression, but Excel 365 Basic does not include Solver or the Analysis ToolPak. Instead, we use a simple linear model that Excel can compute directly. This model produces a numeric score that increases for customers who look more likely to respond and decreases for customers who look less likely. Later, we convert this score into a Yes/No prediction using a decision threshold.

To begin, we build a model using only Days Since Last Purchase as the predictor. Excel's builtin LINEST function can estimate a straightline relationship between Days Since Last Purchase and the encoded response (1 for Yes, 0 for No). Although this is not logistic regression, it serves the same purpose in a classification setting: it gives us a datadriven score that we can later convert into a classification.

In an empty twocell row, enter:

=LINEST(F2:F13, B2:B13)

where • F2:F13 contains the encoded responses (1/0), and • B2:B13 contains Days Since Last Purchase.

Excel returns two numbers:

- the slope, and
- the intercept.

These values define the model:

Score = Intercept + Slope × Days Since Last Purchase

Next, create a new column labeled Model Score. If the intercept is in H2 and the slope is in H3, and B2 contains Days Since Last Purchase, enter:

=$H$2 + $H$3 * B2

Copy this down for all twelve customers. This produces a raw score that increases or decreases based on recency.

Because linear scores can fall outside the 0–1 range, we convert them into a probabilitystyle value by clipping them between 0 and 1. In a new column labeled Predicted Probability, enter:

=MAX(0, MIN(1, [ModelScoreCell]))

This ensures all predicted values fall between 0 and 1, just like logistic regression probabilities.

The resulting probabilities now behave exactly as needed for classification: customers with fewer days since their last purchase receive higher predicted probabilities, and customers who have been inactive for a long time receive lower ones. Once you have a predicted probability for each customer, you need to turn that probability into an actual Yes/No prediction. Businesses cannot act on a probability alone—they need a decision. The simplest way to do this is to choose a cutoff value, called a threshold. A common choice is 0.50. If a customer's predicted probability is 0.50 or higher, we classify them as "Yes," meaning the model believes they are likely to respond. If the probability is below 0.50, we classify them as "No." In Excel, this is done with a simple IF statement. If the predicted probability is in H2, the formula is:

=IF(H2>=0.5,"Yes","No")

Copy this down for all customers. This converts the model's numeric output into a practical classification that can be compared to the actual responses. In the next step, you will use these predicted Yes/No values to build a confusion matrix and calculate accuracy, precision, and recall.

Customer	Days Since Last Purchase	Email Opens (Last Month)	Avg Order Value ($)	Responded to Email Campaign?
A	15	8	75	Yes
B	120	0	45	No
C	45	3	120	No
...	...	...	...	...
L	25	6	85	Yes

Customer	Encoded Response (Binary)	Model Score	Predicted Probability	Predicted Class
A	1	0.82	0.82	Yes
B	0	0.14	0.14	No
C	0	0.63	0.63	Yes
...	...	...	...	...
L	1	0.75	0.75	Yes

Once you have the Actual responses and the Predicted responses, you can summarize the model's performance using a confusion matrix. Create a small 2×2 table with Actual values as rows and Predicted values as columns. Then fill each cell using COUNTIFS.

If Actual responses are in column E and Predicted responses are in column I, enter the following formulas:

Actual Yes / Predicted Yes =COUNTIFS(E2:E13,"Yes", I2:I13,"Yes")

Actual Yes / Predicted No =COUNTIFS(E2:E13,"Yes", I2:I13,"No")

Actual No / Predicted Yes =COUNTIFS(E2:E13,"No", I2:I13,"Yes")

Actual No / Predicted No =COUNTIFS(E2:E13,"No", I2:I13,"No")

Using your data, the completed confusion matrix is:

Table 5.13: Confusion matrix for classification model

Actual Predicted	Predicted Yes	Predicted No
Actual Yes	6	0
Actual No	2	4

This matrix shows that the model correctly predicted 6 responders and 4 nonresponders, with 2 false positives and no false negatives.

5.12.1.3 Step 3: Expand the model to multiple inputs

So far, the model has used only Days Since Last Purchase to generate a prediction score. Excel 365 Basic can also create a score that uses multiple predictors at the same time. This allows the model to consider more information about each customer, such as Email Opens and Average Order Value, and usually improves prediction accuracy.

To build a multiinput model, use the LINEST function again, but this time include all three predictors. In an empty row with three cells available for the coefficients and one for the intercept, enter:

=LINEST(F2:F13, B2:D13, TRUE, FALSE)

Here, F2:F13 contains the encoded responses, and B2:D13 contains the three predictors. Excel returns four values: one coefficient for each predictor and one intercept. Using your data, the results are:

- Coefficient for Days Since Last Purchase: −0.00614167
- Coefficient for Email Opens: 0.159950758
- Coefficient for Average Order Value: −0.001819337

- Intercept: 0.419459146

These values define the multiinput model:

Score = 0.419459146 + (−0.00614167 × Days Since Last Purchase) + (0.159950758 × Email Opens) + (−0.001819337 × Average Order Value)

Create a new column labeled MultiInput Score. If the intercept and coefficients are stored in H2 through H5, and the predictors for the first customer are in B2, C2, and D2, enter:

=$H$2 + $H$3*B2 + $H$4*C2 + $H$5*D2

The multiinput model produces a score that can be positive or negative. To turn this into a probabilitystyle value between 0 and 1, use the same clipping formula as before. If the multiinput score is in column G, enter:

=MAX(0, MIN(1, G2))

Copy this down for all customers. This gives you a probability between 0 and 1 for each row.

Next, convert the probability into a Yes/No prediction using the same 0.50 threshold. If the probability is in H2, enter:

=IF(H2>=0.5,"Yes","No")

Copy this down. This produces the final predicted class for the multiinput model.

Customer	Days Since Last Purchase	Email Opens (Last Month)	Avg Order Value ($)	Responded?	Encoded Response
A	15	8	75	Yes	1
B	120	0	45	No	0
…	…	…	…	…	…
L	25	6	85	Yes	1

Customer	MultiInput Score	Probability	Prediction
A	1.47	1.00	Yes
B	-0.40	0.00	No
…	…	…	…
L	1.07	1.00	Yes

Once you have the Actual responses and the Predicted responses from the multiinput model, you can summarize performance the same way as before. Create a 2×2 table with Actual values as rows and Predicted values as columns. Use the same COUNTIFS formulas, just referencing the new Predicted column.

If Actual responses are in column E and the new multivariate Predicted values are in column I, enter:

Actual Yes / Predicted Yes =COUNTIFS(E2:E13,"Yes", I2:I13,"Yes")

Actual Yes / Predicted No =COUNTIFS(E2:E13,"Yes", I2:I13,"No")

Actual No / Predicted Yes =COUNTIFS(E2:E13,"No", I2:I13,"Yes")

Actual No / Predicted No =COUNTIFS(E2:E13,"No", I2:I13,"No")

Using multivariate predictions, the confusion matrix is:

Table 5.16: Confusion matrix for classification model

Actual Predicted	Predicted Yes	Predicted No
Actual Yes	6	0
Actual No	0	6

This means the multiinput model correctly classified all 12 customers with no errors.

5.12.2 Practice

A subscription service wants to predict whether a customer will renew their subscription next month. The dataset contains behavioral and demographic information.

Table 5.17: Customer retention and support interaction dataset

Customer	Days Since Last Login	Support Calls (Last Month)	Avg Monthly Spend ($)	Renewed?
1	5	0	75	Yes
2	50	1	50	No
3	2	0	120	Yes
...	...	...	...	...
20	50	2	55	No

5.12.2.1 Questions

1. Use LINEST to build the single-input model using Days Since Last Purchase as the only predictor. Record the slope and intercept returned by Excel.
2. Calculate the single-input prediction score for all 12 customers using the slope and intercept you obtained.
3. Convert the single-input scores into predicted probabilities by clipping values below 0 to 0 and values above 1 to 1.

4. Apply the 0.50 threshold to generate a Yes/No prediction for each customer using the single-input model.
5. Create the confusion matrix for the single-input model using COUNTIFS and report the four counts:
6. Calculate accuracy, precision, and recall for the single-input model based on your confusion matrix.
7. Use LINEST again to build the multi-input model using all three predictors (Days Since Last Purchase, Email Opens, and Average Order Value). Record the three coefficients and the intercept.
8. Calculate the multi-input prediction score for all 12 customers using the multivariate coefficients.
9. Convert the multi-input scores into probabilities and apply the 0.50 threshold to generate the final Yes/No predictions for the multi-input model.
10. Create the confusion matrix for the multi-input model

Chapter 6

Communicating Results

6.1 Learning Outcomes

6-1. Recognize how to tell simple stories with business data using context, insights, and recommendations

6-2. Understand basic ways to show data that help business people make decisions

6-3. Identify how to write clear business messages that explain what data means

6-4. Recognize how computers can help make data communication easier and more effective

6.2 Introduction

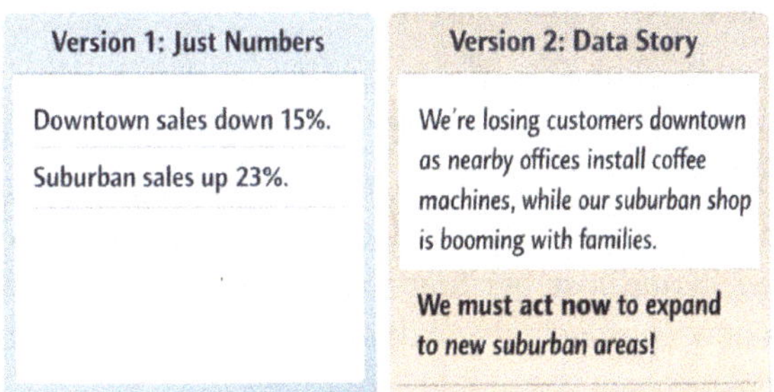

Imagine you work for a small coffee shop chain, and after weeks of analyzing sales data, you've discovered something important: the downtown location is losing customers every month, while the suburban location is growing rapidly. You have charts, numbers, and detailed analysis that prove this trend. But now comes the hardest part - you need to explain this to your boss in a way that makes sense and motivates action.

This is what data storytelling is all about. It's not enough to find interesting patterns in data - you need to communicate those patterns in ways that help people understand what's happening and what they should do about it. Think of it like being a translator who takes the language of numbers and charts and turns it into the language of business decisions.

Every day, businesses generate enormous amounts of data about their customers, sales, operations, and performance. But data by itself doesn't make decisions - people do. And people need stories, not just statistics, to understand what the data means for their business. A good data story can be the difference between important insights being ignored and those same insights driving real business improvements.

Consider the difference between these two ways of presenting the same information. Version 1 (Just Numbers): "Downtown location sales decreased 15% over 6 months. Suburban location sales increased 23% over the same period. Customer traffic patterns show different demographic preferences." Version 2 (Data Story): "Our downtown coffee shop is in trouble. We're losing about 50 customers per month because nearby office buildings have installed their own coffee machines, and workers don't need to come to us anymore. Meanwhile, our suburban location is thriving because families in that area love our kid-friendly atmosphere and weekend events. If we don't act soon, we could lose $80,000 in revenue this year from the downtown location. But we have an opportunity to expand our family-focused approach to other suburban areas."

The second version tells a story that helps people understand not just what's happening, but why it's happening and what it means for the business. This is the power of data storytelling. Modern technology has made data analysis easier than ever, but it has also made effective communication more important. Business managers are overwhelmed with reports, dashboards, and data from every department. The people who can turn that flood of information into clear, actionable stories are the ones who get their recommendations implemented and their careers advanced.

In this module, we'll learn how to transform data analysis into compelling business stories. We'll explore a simple framework for organizing data stories, understand how to create visuals that support decision-making, learn to write clear business communications, and discover how modern tools can help make data communication more effective. Whether you're presenting to your boss, writing a report for your team, or trying to convince colleagues to try a new approach, the skills in this module will help you turn your data insights into business impact.

6.3 The Simple Framework for Data Stories

6.3.1 The Three Parts Every Data Story Needs

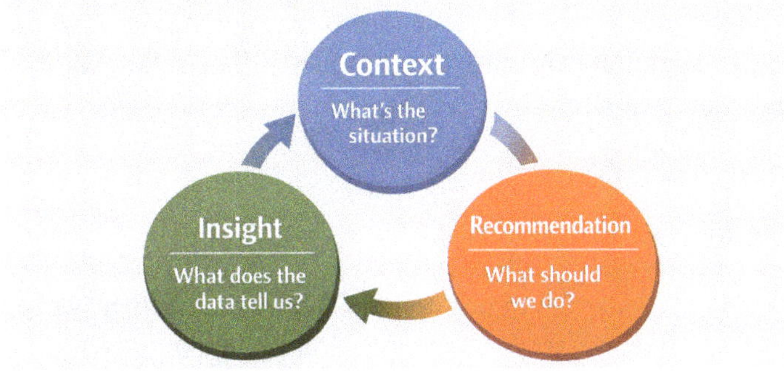

Every effective data story has three essential parts that work together to help people understand and act on information. Think of these parts like the beginning, middle, and end of any good story - each part has a specific job to do, and they work together to create a complete message that motivates action.

The first part is Context. This explains the situation and why the data matters. Context answers the question "Why should I care about this?" It sets up the business problem or opportunity that the data analysis is trying to address. Without good context, even the most interesting data insights can seem irrelevant or confusing to busy managers.

The second part is Insight. This explains what the data shows and what it means for the business. Insights go beyond just reporting numbers to explain what those numbers mean for business performance, customer behavior, or operational efficiency. Good insights are surprising enough to get attention but clear enough to understand quickly.

The third part is Recommendation. This explains what should be done based on the insights. Recommendations translate data insights into specific actions that address the business situation described in the context. They should be concrete enough that people know exactly what to do next.

Let's look at how this framework works with a real business example. Imagine you're analyzing customer service data for a small online store. Context: "Our customer service team has been overwhelmed lately, with response times getting longer and customer complaints increasing. We need to understand what's causing these problems so we can fix them before we start losing customers to competitors." Insight: "Our analysis shows that 60% of customer service requests are about the same three issues: order tracking, return policies, and product sizing. These are all questions that customers could answer themselves if they had better information on our website. Meanwhile, our service team is spending 4 hours per day answering these repetitive questions instead of helping customers with complex problems." Recommendation: "We should create a comprehensive FAQ section and improve our product pages with better sizing information and clear return policies. This would reduce routine inquiries by about

60%, allowing our service team to focus on customers who really need personal help. We estimate this would improve response times from 8 hours to 3 hours and reduce customer complaints by 40%."

This framework works because it mirrors how people naturally think about business problems. First, they want to understand the situation (context). Then they want to know what the data reveals about that situation (insight). Finally, they want to know what to do about it (recommendation).

6.3.2 Making Context Clear and Compelling

The context section of your data story is crucial because it determines whether people will pay attention to the rest of your message. If people don't understand why the analysis matters, they won't care about your insights or recommendations, no matter how brilliant they are.

Good context explains the business situation in terms that matter to your audience. It should describe the problem or opportunity, explain why it's important to address now, and set up the stakes involved. Think about what keeps your audience awake at night - those are the business concerns that make for compelling context.

For a retail business analyzing seasonal sales patterns, weak context might sound like: "We analyzed sales data from the past year to identify seasonal trends." This doesn't explain why anyone should care about seasonal trends or what business problem this analysis addresses.

Strong context for the same analysis might sound like: "Our inventory costs have increased 25% this year because we keep ordering too much of some products and running out of others. With the holiday season approaching, we need to understand our seasonal sales patterns so we can order the right amounts and avoid both stockouts and excess inventory that hurts our profits."

The strong context explains not just what was analyzed, but why it matters for business performance and what's at stake if the problem isn't solved. It creates urgency and relevance that captures attention and prepares people to receive the insights.

Context should also be appropriate for your audience. Executives care about financial impact and strategic implications. Operations managers care about efficiency and resource allocation. Sales teams care about customer relationships and revenue opportunities. The same data analysis might require different context depending on who you're talking to.

6.3.3 Turning Data into Clear Insights

Insights are the heart of data storytelling because they explain what the data means for business. But creating good insights requires going beyond just reporting what the numbers show to explaining what those numbers mean for business performance and decision-making.

Weak insights simply report what the data show: "Sales increased 15% in the third quarter." This is just a fact. It doesn't explain what this means for the business or why it happened.

Strong insights explain what the data means: "Sales increased 15% in the third quarter, primarily because our new customer referral program brought in 200 new customers who spent an average of $150 each. This suggests that word-of-mouth marketing is more effective for our business than traditional advertising, and we should consider expanding referral incentives."

Good insights have several characteristics that make them valuable for business decision-making. They are surprising and reveal something unexpected that challenges existing assumptions or explains puzzling performance. For example, "We thought our website problems were hurting sales, but the data shows that customers who experience website issues actually spend 20% more because they call our sales team directly."

They are relevant and address business concerns that matter for pending decisions or strategic planning. "Customer acquisition costs are highest for social media advertising but lowest for email marketing to existing customers, which affects how we should allocate our marketing budget."

They are actionable and suggest specific responses or point toward particular solutions. "Customers who use our mobile app place orders 40% more frequently than website-only customers, suggesting we should invest more in app development and promotion."

Let's look at a complete example of how to turn data into insights. A restaurant analyzing customer feedback might discover that complaints spike on weekends. Here's how to turn this observation into a valuable insight. Data Observation: "Customer complaints are 60% higher on weekends than weekdays." Business Insight: "Weekend complaints are 60% higher than weekdays because we're understaffed during our busiest periods. Most complaints are about slow service and long wait times, not food quality. This suggests that our weekend staffing model isn't matching customer demand, and we're losing potential revenue because customers leave before ordering or don't return due to poor service experiences."

The insight explains not just what's happening (more complaints on weekends) but why it's happening (understaffing during busy periods) and what it means for the business (lost revenue and customer retention problems).

6.3.4 Creating Actionable Recommendations

Recommendations are where data stories translate insights into specific actions that address the business situation. Good recommendations are concrete enough that people know exactly what to do, feasible enough that they can actually be implemented, and directly connected to the insights presented.

Weak recommendations are vague and don't provide clear guidance: "We should improve customer service." This doesn't tell anyone what specific actions to take or how to measure success.

Strong recommendations are specific and actionable: "We should hire two additional servers for weekend shifts and implement a reservation system to better manage customer flow. This would reduce average wait times from 25 minutes to 15 minutes and should decrease weekend complaints by 50%. The additional staff would cost $800 per month but should increase weekend revenue by $3,000 through better customer retention and higher table turnover."

Effective recommendations include several key elements. They specify exactly what actions to take, making it clear who should do what and when. They predict the expected results, explaining how the recommended actions will address the business problem identified in the context. They provide a business case that explains why the recommended actions are worth the investment of time, money, or resources required.

Good recommendations also acknowledge potential challenges or limitations. They might say something like: "This approach requires training our current staff on the new reservation system, which will take about two weeks to implement fully. We should also monitor customer feedback closely during the transition to ensure the new system improves rather than complicates the dining experience."

The best recommendations make it easy for decision-makers to say yes. They provide enough detail that people can visualize how the solution would work, enough justification that people understand why it's worth doing, and enough specificity that people know exactly what steps to take next.

6.4 Effective Data Visualization for Business Communication

6.4.1 Choosing the Right Visual for Your Message

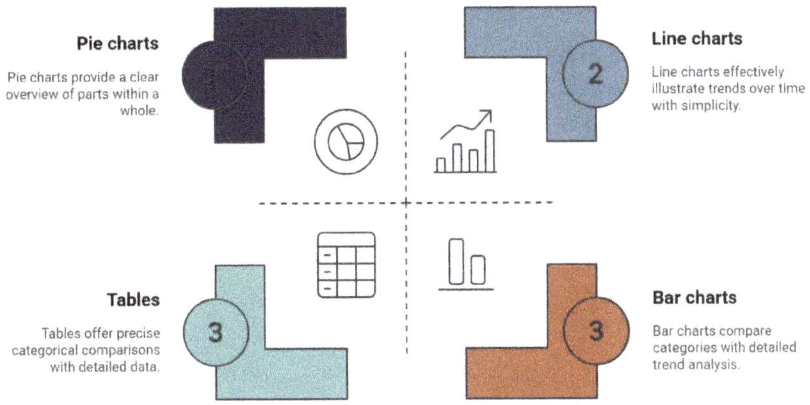

Data visualization is a powerful tool for business communication, but only when the right type of chart or graph is matched to the message you're trying to convey. Different types of data and different business questions require different visual approaches. The key is understanding what story your data tells and choosing visuals that make that story clear and compelling.

When you want to show how something changes over time, line charts are usually your best choice. They make trends, patterns, and changes easy to see at a glance. For example, if you're showing how website traffic has grown over the past year, a line chart will clearly display the upward trend and any seasonal variations. Bar charts work well when you want to compare different categories or groups. If you're comparing sales performance across different product lines or regions, bar charts make it easy to see which categories are performing better than others.

Pie charts should be used sparingly and only when you want to show how parts relate to a whole. They work best when you have just a few categories that add up to 100% of something. For instance, showing what percentage of your budget goes to different expense categories. However, pie charts become confusing when you have too many small slices or when the differences between slices are subtle.

Tables are excellent for presenting precise numbers when your audience needs to see exact values rather than general trends. They're particularly useful for financial data, detailed comparisons, or when people need to look up specific information. However, tables can be overwhelming if they contain too much information, so use them strategically.

The most important principle in choosing visuals is to match the chart type to your business message. If you want to emphasize growth, use a line chart that shows the upward trend. If you want to highlight which product is your best seller, use a bar chart that makes the comparison obvious. If you want to show market share, a pie chart might be appropriate if you have just a few major competitors.

6.4.2 Making Visuals Clear and Professional

Once you've chosen the right type of visual, you need to make sure it communicates clearly and looks professional. Clear visuals help your audience understand your message quickly, while confusing or cluttered visuals can undermine even the best insights.

Start with clear, descriptive titles that tell people what they're looking at. Instead of "Sales Data," use "Monthly Sales Revenue Shows 15% Growth in Q3." The title should summarize the main message of the chart so people understand the key point even before they study the details.

Label your axes clearly and include units of measurement. If you're showing dollar amounts, make sure the axis says "Revenue (in thousands)" or whatever unit you're using. If you're showing percentages, make that clear too. Don't make people guess what the numbers represent.

Use colors strategically to highlight important information. You might use your company's brand colors for consistency, or use contrasting colors to emphasize key data points. However, avoid using too many colors, which can make charts look cluttered and confusing. Stick to a simple color palette that serves your message.

Keep charts simple and focused. Remove unnecessary gridlines, borders, or decorative elements that don't add to understanding. The goal is to make your data the star, not the chart design. Every element in your visual should either help people understand the data or be removed.

Make sure your visuals are large enough to read easily, whether they're being viewed on a computer screen or printed on paper. Test your charts by viewing them at the size they'll actually be used. If people have to squint to read the labels, the chart won't be effective.

Consider your audience when designing visuals. Executives might prefer high-level summary charts that show the big picture, while operational managers might need more detailed breakdowns. Financial audiences will expect precise numbers and clear methodologies, while marketing teams might respond better to visuals that emphasize trends and opportunities.

6.4.3 Using Visuals to Support Decision-Making

The ultimate goal of business data visualization is to support better decision-making. This means your visuals should not just display data, but help people understand what the data means for their decisions and actions.

One effective approach is to use annotations or callouts to highlight key insights directly on your charts. For example, if your sales chart shows a significant spike in a particular month, add a note explaining what caused that spike. This helps people understand not just what happened, but why it happened.

Consider creating before-and-after comparisons when you're proposing changes or showing the impact of past decisions. These comparisons make it easy for people to see the potential benefits of taking action. For instance, you might show customer satisfaction scores before and after implementing a new service process.

Use visual hierarchy to guide people's attention to the most important information first. Make key data points larger, bolder, or in contrasting colors. Arrange multiple charts so that the most important message is prominent and supporting details are secondary.

When presenting multiple related charts, make sure they work together to tell a coherent story. Each chart should build on the previous one, leading your audience through your analysis toward your recommendations. Think of your visuals as chapters in a book - each one should advance the overall narrative.

Consider including trend lines or benchmarks that help people interpret whether performance is good or bad. For example, if you're showing monthly sales figures, include a trend line that shows whether sales are generally increasing or decreasing. If you're showing customer satisfaction scores, include industry benchmarks so people can see how your company compares to competitors.

6.5 Writing Clear Business Messages About Data

6.5.1 Structuring Data-Driven Reports and Presentations

Writing effective business messages about data requires a clear structure that guides readers through your analysis and toward your recommendations. The structure should feel logical and natural, making it easy for busy managers to find the information they need and understand what actions to take.

Start with an executive summary that captures the most important points in just a few paragraphs. Many executives will only read this section, so it needs to include your key findings and primary recommendations. The executive summary should be able to stand alone as a complete message, even though the rest of the document provides supporting details.

After the executive summary, provide the context that explains why this analysis matters. This section should describe the business situation, explain what prompted the analysis, and set up the stakes involved. Help readers understand why they should care about this particular data and what business problems or opportunities it addresses.

Present your methodology briefly but clearly. You don't need to include every technical detail, but you should explain how the data was collected, what time period it covers, and any important limitations or assumptions. This builds credibility and helps readers understand how much confidence to place in your findings.

Organize your findings in order of importance, starting with the most significant insights. Each major finding should be clearly stated, supported with specific data, and explained in terms of what it means for the business. Use subheadings to make it easy for readers to scan the document and find specific information.

End with clear, specific recommendations that directly address the business situation described in your context. Each recommendation should be actionable, feasible, and directly connected to your findings. Include expected outcomes, resource requirements, and suggested timelines when possible.

6.5.2 Writing for Different Business Audiences

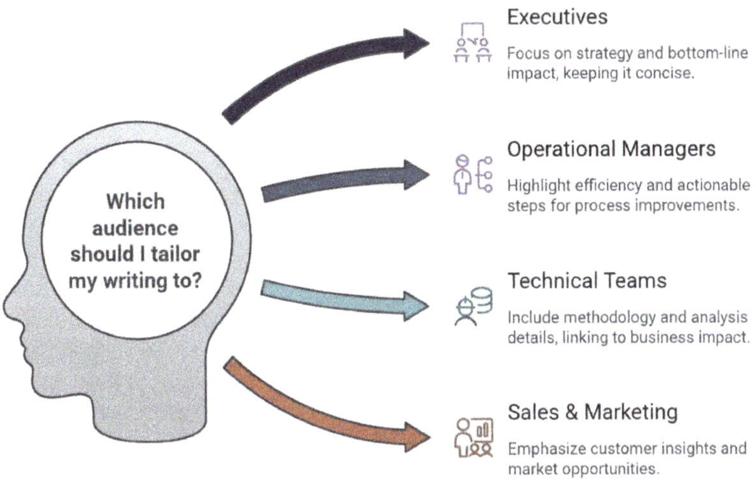

Different business audiences have different information needs, time constraints, and decision-making responsibilities. Effective data communication requires adapting your message to match your audience's priorities and communication preferences.

When writing for executives, focus on strategic implications and bottom-line impact. Executives want to understand how your findings affect company performance, competitive position, or strategic goals. They typically have limited time, so get to the point quickly and emphasize financial impact, risk management, or growth opportunities. Use language that connects data insights to business strategy and long-term success.

For operational managers, emphasize efficiency, process improvements, and resource allocation. These audiences want to understand how your findings affect day-to-day operations and what specific changes they should make to improve performance. Include practical details about implementation, staffing requirements, or process changes. Use language that focuses on operational excellence and continuous improvement.

When communicating with technical teams, you can include more methodological detail and statistical analysis. These audiences appreciate understanding how the analysis was conducted and may want to replicate or extend your work. However, still focus on business implications rather than just technical findings. Explain what the technical results mean for business performance and decision-making.

For sales and marketing teams, emphasize customer insights, market opportunities, and competitive advantages. These audiences want to understand how your findings can help them better serve customers, identify new opportunities, or improve their effectiveness. Use language that connects data insights to customer needs and market dynamics.

Regardless of your audience, always lead with business impact rather than technical details. Start with what the data means for business performance, then provide supporting details as needed. Use concrete examples and specific numbers to make abstract concepts tangible and memorable.

6.5.3 Making Complex Data Accessible

One of the biggest challenges in business data communication is making complex analysis accessible to people who may not have strong analytical backgrounds. The goal is to preserve the accuracy and nuance of your findings while making them understandable to busy professionals who need to make decisions based on your work.

Use analogies and comparisons to make abstract numbers more concrete. Instead of saying "Customer acquisition cost increased 23%," you might say "We're now spending $23 more to acquire each new customer, which is like adding an extra $2,300 to our monthly marketing budget for every 100 new customers we gain."

Break complex findings into smaller, digestible pieces. If you've discovered multiple related insights, present them one at a time rather than trying to explain everything at once. Use bullet points, numbered lists, or short paragraphs to make information easy to scan and absorb.

Define technical terms and explain analytical concepts when necessary, but do so briefly and in business language. For example, instead of discussing "statistical significance," you might say "We can be confident that this difference is real and not just due to random variation in the data."

Use specific examples to illustrate general findings. If your analysis shows that customer satisfaction varies by region, include a specific example: "For instance, customers in the Northeast rate our service 4.2 out of 5, while customers in the Southwest rate it 3.6 out of 5." Specific examples make general patterns more concrete and memorable.

Anticipate questions and objections your audience might have, and address them proactively. If your recommendations require significant investment, acknowledge the costs upfront and explain why the benefits justify the expense. If your findings contradict conventional wisdom, explain why the data suggests a different conclusion.

Focus on implications rather than methodology. While it's important to establish credibility, most business audiences care more about what the findings mean for their decisions than about how the analysis was conducted. Lead with business implications and provide methodological details only when they're necessary for understanding or credibility.

6.6 Technology Tools for Data Communication

6.6.1 Modern Platforms for Creating Data Stories

Technology has revolutionized how we create and share data stories, making it easier than ever to combine analysis, visualization, and narrative into compelling business communications. Modern platforms offer powerful capabilities that can help even non-technical users create professional, interactive data presentations.

Business intelligence platforms like Tableau, Power BI, and Qlik Sense allow users to create interactive dashboards and reports that combine multiple data sources, sophisticated visualizations, and narrative elements. These platforms make it possible to create data stories that readers can explore themselves, drilling down into details that interest them most. For example, an executive might start with a high-level sales summary and then click through to see performance by region, product line, or time period.

Presentation software has evolved beyond simple slide decks to support rich, interactive content. Tools like Prezi, Canva, and even advanced PowerPoint features allow you to create presentations that combine data visualizations, animations, and storytelling elements in engaging ways. These tools make it easier to guide audiences through complex data stories while maintaining their attention and interest.

Cloud-based collaboration platforms like Google Workspace, Microsoft 365, and Slack integration tools enable teams to work together on data stories, share feedback, and iterate quickly. These platforms make it possible to involve stakeholders in the story development process, ensuring that the final message resonates with its intended audience.

Specialized data storytelling platforms like Flourish, DataWrapper, and Infogram focus specifically on creating compelling visual narratives from data. These tools often include templates and guided workflows that help users structure their data stories effectively, even if they don't have extensive design or analytical experience.

The key to choosing the right platform is understanding your audience, your technical capabilities, and your communication goals. If you're creating a one-time presentation for executives, a sophisticated slide deck might be perfect. If you're building ongoing reporting for operational managers, an interactive dashboard might be more appropriate.

6.6.2 Automation and Efficiency in Data Communication

As businesses generate more data and need more frequent reporting, automation becomes crucial for efficient data communication. Modern tools can automate many aspects of data story creation, from data collection and analysis to visualization and distribution.

Automated reporting tools can pull data from multiple sources, perform standard analyses, and generate regular reports without manual intervention. This is particularly valuable for routine business reporting like monthly sales summaries, weekly operational metrics, or quarterly performance reviews. Automation ensures consistency, reduces errors, and frees up time for more strategic analysis and communication.

Template-based systems allow organizations to standardize their data communication while still allowing for customization. For example, a company might create standard templates for different types of analysis - market research, operational performance, financial analysis - that ensure consistent structure and branding while allowing analysts to focus on insights rather than formatting.

Real-time dashboards and alerts can automatically notify stakeholders when important metrics change or when data reveals significant trends. This enables faster response to business opportunities or problems, turning data communication from a periodic activity into an ongoing business capability.

Machine learning and artificial intelligence are beginning to assist with data storytelling by automatically identifying patterns, generating insights, and even suggesting narrative structures. While these technologies are still developing, they show promise for helping analysts focus on interpretation and recommendation rather than pattern detection.

However, automation should enhance rather than replace human judgment in data communication. The most important aspects of data storytelling - understanding business context, interpreting what data means for decision-making, and crafting compelling recommendations - still require human insight and business knowledge.

6.6.3 Best Practices for Digital Data Presentation

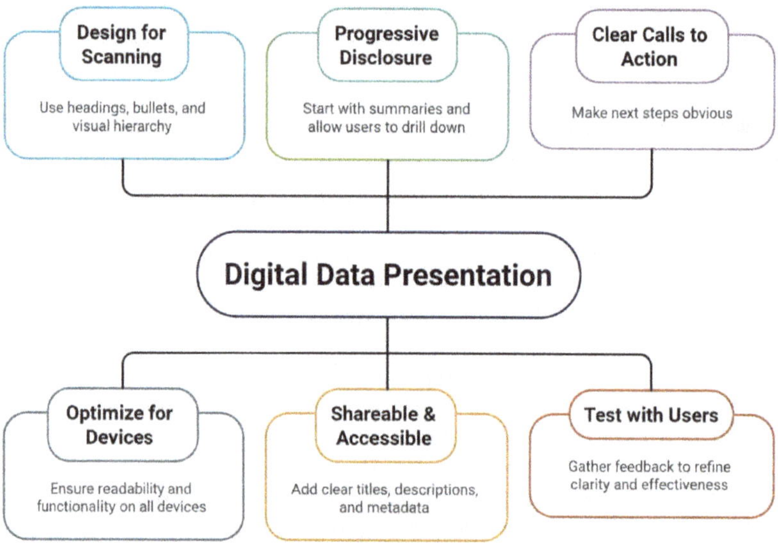

Digital presentation of data stories offers unique opportunities and challenges compared to traditional printed reports or in-person presentations. Understanding how people consume digital content can help you create more effective data communications.

Design for scanning rather than reading. Online audiences typically scan content quickly, looking for key points and interesting visuals. Use clear headings, bullet points, and visual hierarchy to make your most important messages easy to find. Place key insights and recommendations prominently where they'll be noticed even by readers who don't read every word.

Optimize for different devices and screen sizes. Your data story might be viewed on everything from smartphones to large desktop monitors. Test your content on different devices to ensure that charts are readable, text is legible, and interactive elements work properly across platforms.

Use progressive disclosure to manage information complexity. Start with high-level summaries and allow readers to drill down into details as needed. This approach serves both executives who want quick overviews and operational managers who need detailed information for implementation.

Make content shareable and accessible. Include clear titles, descriptions, and metadata that make it easy for people to find and share your work. Consider how your data story will look when shared via email, social media, or collaboration platforms.

Include clear calls to action that tell readers what to do next. Whether you want them to approve a budget, change a process, or conduct additional analysis, make the next steps obvious and easy to follow.

Test your digital presentations with real users before wide distribution. What seems clear to you as the creator might be confusing to your intended audience. Getting feedback early can help you refine your message and improve its effectiveness.

Remember that digital data stories can be updated and improved over time. Unlike printed reports, digital content can be revised based on feedback, updated with new data, or enhanced with additional analysis. Build this flexibility into your planning and be prepared to iterate based on how your audience responds to your initial version.

6.7 Conclusion

Effective data storytelling is one of the most valuable skills in modern business. As organizations generate more data and face more complex decisions, the ability to transform analysis into compelling, actionable stories becomes increasingly important for career success and business impact.

The framework we've explored - context, insights, and recommendations - provides a simple but powerful structure for organizing data communications. By starting with clear context that explains why the analysis matters, developing insights that explain what the data means for business performance, and ending with specific recommendations that guide action, you can create data stories that drive real business results.

Remember that technology is a tool to enhance your storytelling, not replace the fundamental need for clear thinking and effective communication. The best data visualization software in the world won't help if you haven't first understood your audience, clarified your message, and structured your story effectively.

Practice these skills regularly, seek feedback from your colleagues, and pay attention to which approaches work best with different audiences and situations. Data storytelling is both an art and a science - the technical skills can be learned, but the judgment about what stories to tell and how to tell them develops through experience and reflection.

As you develop these capabilities, you'll find that data storytelling becomes not just a way to present analysis, but a way to think more clearly about business problems and opportunities. The discipline of structuring data stories forces you to clarify your thinking, test your assumptions, and focus on what really matters for business success.

The organizations and individuals who master data storytelling will have significant advantages in our increasingly data-driven business environment. They'll be able to cut through information overload, focus attention on what matters most, and drive action that creates real business value. These are the skills that turn data into decisions and analysis into impact.

6.8 Key Terns

Data storytelling – The practice of turning data analysis into a clear, compelling narrative that helps people understand insights and take action.

Context – The background information that explains why the data matters and sets up the business problem or opportunity.

Insight – An interpretation of data that explains what the numbers mean for business performance, behavior, or decisions.

Recommendation – A specific, actionable suggestion for what to do based on insights from the data.

Business communication – The process of conveying information effectively to help stakeholders make informed decisions.

Data visualization – The graphical representation of data using charts, graphs, or tables to make information easier to understand.

Line charts – Visuals that show trends or changes over time, useful for highlighting patterns.

Bar charts – Visuals that compare categories or groups to show differences or rankings clearly.

Pie charts – Visuals that show parts of a whole, best used for a few distinct categories that sum to 100%.

Tables – Structured grids of data that provide precise numerical information for detailed analysis or comparison.

Executive summary – A concise overview of key findings and recommendations, often read by decision-makers first.

Audience adaptation – Tailoring the presentation of data and insights to meet the priorities and knowledge level of different stakeholders.

Digital presentation – Delivering data stories online or on screens, using interactive or visual elements suited for digital consumption.

Progressive disclosure – A design approach that presents high-level summaries first, with options to explore more detailed information as needed.

Automation – The use of tools to collect, analyze, visualize, and distribute data reports with minimal manual effort.

Interactive dashboards – Digital interfaces that allow users to explore data, filter views, and drill down into details dynamically.

Call to action – A clear statement telling the audience what action they should take based on the data insights.

Clarity and simplicity – Ensuring visuals, text, and recommendations are easy to understand and focus on key messages.

Methodology – The approach and processes used to collect and analyze data, which supports credibility and understanding.

Business impact – The effect that insights, decisions, or actions have on organizational performance, revenue, efficiency, or growth.

6.9 Review Questions

1. Explain the three parts of a data story and why each is important.
2. How does context influence the effectiveness of a data story? Give an example.
3. What makes an insight "strong" rather than just a data observation?
4. List three characteristics of actionable recommendations in business communication.
5. How should you choose the right visual to match your business message? Provide examples.
6. Describe how you would adapt a data report for executives versus operational managers.
7. What are some best practices for digital presentation of data stories?
8. How can technology tools enhance data communication, and what limitations do they have?

6.10 Lab 6-1 Communicating Data Insights

This lab focuses on the part of analytics that matters most in real business settings: turning numbers into a clear, persuasive story. You'll work with a small sales dataset, use Excel to surface meaningful patterns, and then translate those findings into charts and written insights that a manager can act on. The goal is not just to analyze data, but to communicate it—using context, insight, and recommendation to show what's happening, why it matters, and what should happen next.

6.10.1 Demonstration

Table 6.1: Regional monthly sales and customer activity metrics

Location	Month	Sales	Customers	Avg Order	New Customers	Complaints	Weekend Visits	Promotion
Downtown	Jan	24500	720	34.03	150	12	210	Yes
Downtown	Feb	23800	690	34.49	140	15	190	No
Downtown	Mar	23050	670	34.43	135	18	185	Yes
Downtown	Apr	22200	640	34.69	120	20	170	No
Downtown	May	21000	600	35.00	110	22	150	Yes
Downtown	Jun	20500	580	35.34	100	25	140	No
Suburban	Jan	18500	520	35.58	130	8	200	Yes
Suburban	Feb	19500	540	36.11	140	7	220	No
Suburban	Mar	20550	580	35.43	150	9	230	Yes
Suburban	Apr	21500	620	34.68	160	10	250	No
Suburban	May	22500	660	34.09	180	12	270	Yes
Suburban	Jun	24000	700	34.29	190	15	300	No

6.10.1.1 Step 1: Tell stories with summary statistics

Begin by creating a PivotTable that summarizes the two locations side by side. Place **Location** in the Rows area and add **Total_Sales**, **Customer_Count**, and **Complaints** to the Values area, changing each field to **Average**. This produces a compact, manager-ready comparison that immediately highlights the performance differences between Downtown and Suburban.

The PivotTable shows that Downtown averages about **$22,508** in monthly sales and serves roughly **650 customers** per month, but it also carries a much higher average complaint level of **18.67**. Suburban, by contrast, averages slightly lower monthly sales at **$21,092** and about **603 customers**, yet its complaint level is almost half of Downtown's at **10.17**. Even before looking at trends, this contrast signals two very different operating environments: Downtown generates more revenue but struggles with customer experience, while Suburban operates more smoothly with fewer issues.

These summary statistics set the stage for the deeper story revealed in the month-to-month data. Downtown's higher averages sit on top of a declining trend, while Suburban's lower averages sit on top of a rising one. The PivotTable doesn't show the trend itself—it shows the **baseline contrast** that makes the trend meaningful. It gives you the snapshot; the next steps explain the motion behind it.

Table 6.2: Average regional performance metrics

Region	Avg Total Sales	Avg Customer Count	Avg Complaints
Downtown	22508.33	650.00	18.67
Suburban	21091.67	603.33	10.17

6.10.1.2 Step 2: Visualize the information

With the PivotTable establishing the high-level contrast between Downtown and Suburban, the next step is to use charts to reveal the *movement* behind those averages. Start by creating a simple line chart of **Total Sales by Month** for each location. This chart immediately shows Downtown sliding downward from January to June, while Suburban climbs steadily over the same period.

A second line chart for **Customer Count by Month** reinforces the same pattern: Downtown loses traffic month after month, and Suburban gains it. These two visuals work together to show that the averages in the PivotTable are not static—they reflect two opposite trajectories.

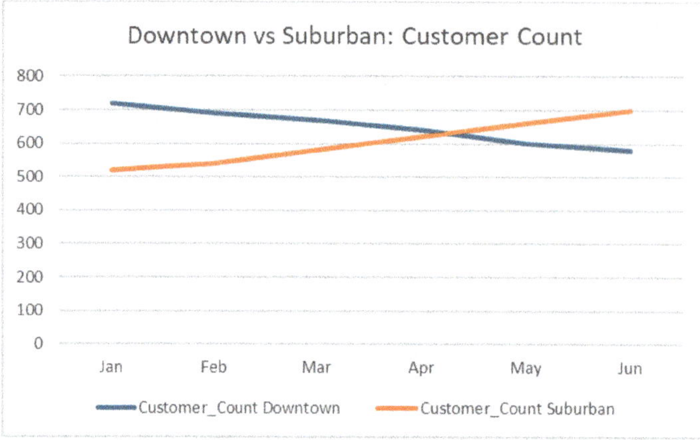

Next, create a bar chart comparing the **average number of complaints** for the two locations. This chart makes the contrast unmistakable: Downtown's complaint levels rise throughout the period and average nearly twice as high as Suburban's. Suburban's complaints remain low and stable, supporting the growth you saw in the line charts.

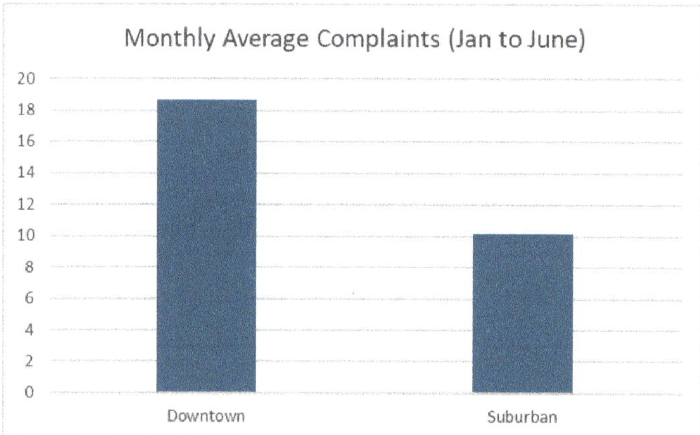

Together, these visuals turn the dataset into a clear narrative: Downtown is declining in sales, traffic, and customer experience, while Suburban is strengthening across all three. The charts don't just display numbers—they reveal the underlying story.

6.10.1.3 Step 3: Business insights and actional recommendation

Across the six-month period, the charts reveal two locations moving in opposite directions. Downtown begins the year with strong sales and high customer traffic, but both lines slope downward month after month. The complaints bar chart reinforces the decline: customer issues rise steadily from January through June, signaling a deteriorating experience that likely contributes to the drop in traffic and revenue. Suburban's visuals tell the reverse story. Its sales line climbs consistently, customer counts rise in parallel, and complaints remain low and stable.

Taken together, the charts point to a clear insight: Downtown is losing momentum due to service-quality problems, while Suburban is gaining momentum through stable operations and stronger customer engagement. The recommendation follows naturally. Downtown needs immediate attention to customer experience—staffing adjustments, service improvements, or targeted promotions to stop the decline. Suburban should reinforce what's working by supporting weekend traffic, expanding loyalty programs, or allocating more resources to sustain its growth.

6.10.1.4 Step 4: Create executive summary

When you write your executive summary, focus on turning the charts and summary statistics into a short, clear story about what is happening at each location. Start by describing the overall pattern you see across the visuals rather than listing numbers. Identify whether each location is improving or declining, and connect the trends across sales, customer count, and complaints. Your goal in the first paragraph is to explain the situation in plain language: what direction each location is moving, how the customer experience appears to be changing, and what the contrast between the two locations suggests. Keep it concise and interpretive—your job is to explain the meaning behind the data, not restate the data itself.

In the second paragraph, move from insight to action by explaining what a manager should do in response to the trends you identified. Base your recommendations directly on the patterns in the charts. If a location is declining, suggest actions that address the likely causes—such as improving service quality, adjusting staffing, or running targeted promotions. If a location is improving, recommend ways to reinforce that momentum, like supporting high-traffic periods or expanding successful programs. Your recommendations should feel like a natural extension of the insights you described, showing that you can not only interpret the data but also translate it into practical next steps.

Executive Summary Report

Downtown vs. Suburban Location Performance

Date:	May 2026	Prepared By:	Strategy & Analytics Team
Period:	January – June 2026	Classification:	Confidential – Internal Use Only

Executive Summary

Our two-location performance review reveals a clear divergence in trajectory. The Downtown location is experiencing declining sales and shrinking customer counts, compounded by a rising volume of customer complaints — signals of eroding brand health in that market. In contrast, the Suburban location shows consistent growth in both sales and customer traffic, supported by a stable and low complaint rate, indicating strong operational performance and customer satisfaction. Leadership attention is warranted to stabilize Downtown while capitalizing on Suburban momentum.

Downtown Sales Change (6 Mo.)	Suburban Sales Change (6 Mo.)	Downtown Complaint Escalation
▼ 22.5%	▲ 37.8%	▲ 95.5%
$142K → $110K	$98K → $135K	22 → 43 monthly incidents

Performance Charts | January – June 2026

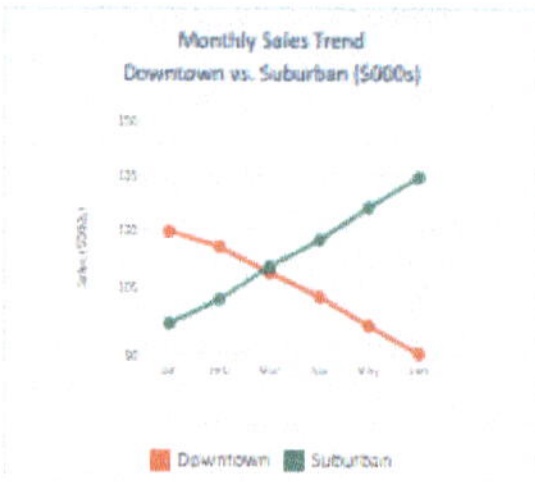

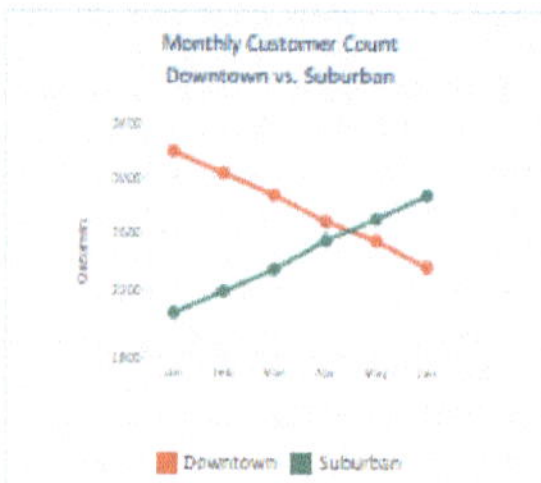

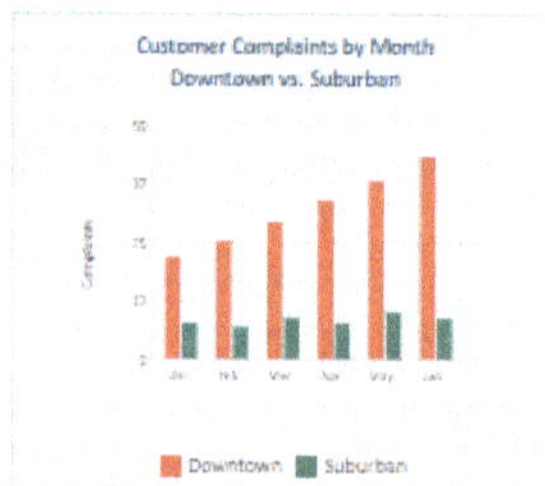

Key Insights

- **Downtown Decline:** Sales dropped ~23% over six months ($142K to $110K), customer count fell ~25%, and complaints nearly doubled — from 22 to 43 monthly incidents.
- **Suburban Growth:** Revenue grew ~38% ($98K to $135K) and customer visits increased ~38%, while complaints remained flat at 7–10 per month.
- **Trajectory Crossover:** Downtown and Suburban customer counts crossed over in April–May, with Suburban now surpassing Downtown in both sales and traffic.

Recommendations

- **Investigate Downtown Root Causes:** Conduct customer exit surveys and staff interviews to identify drivers of declining satisfaction and sales.
- **Reallocate Resources Strategically:** Consider shifting marketing budget and staffing toward the higher-performing Suburban location to maximize ROI.
- **Implement a Downtown Recovery Plan:** Launch a targeted promotional campaign and service improvement initiative at Downtown within 30 days.

6.10.2 Practice

Scenario: A company is evaluating the performance of three different website sections — **Blog**, **Store**, and **Help Center** — over six months. Students will analyze traffic, engagement, and user satisfaction.

Table 6.3: Website performance metrics by section and month

Section	Month	Page Views	Unique Visitors	Avg Time on Page (sec)	Bounce Rate (%)	Conver-sions	Support Tickets
Blog	Jan	42000	18000	92	68	300	12
Blog	Feb	45000	19000	95	66	320	10
Blog	Mar	47000	20000	98	65	340	9
Blog	Apr	46000	19800	96	67	330	11
Blog	May	48000	20500	100	64	360	8
Blog	Jun	50000	21000	102	63	380	7
Store	Jan	38000	15000	75	52	1200	25
Store	Feb	39000	15200	78	51	1250	24
Store	Mar	39500	15500	80	50	1300	23
Store	Apr	40000	15800	82	49	1350	22
Store	May	41000	16000	83	48	1400	21
Store	Jun	42000	16500	85	47	1450	20
Help Center	Jan	30000	14000	110	40	0	320
Help Center	Feb	31000	14500	112	39	0	310
Help Center	Mar	32000	15000	115	38	0	300
Help Center	Apr	33000	15200	118	37	0	290
Help Center	May	34000	15500	120	36	0	280
Help Center	Jun	35000	15800	122	35	0	270

6.10.2.1 Questions

1. Create a PivotTable comparing Blog, Store, and Help Center on average Page Views, Avg Time on Page, and Bounce Rate. What high-level differences stand out across the three sections?

2. Build a line chart of Page Views by Month for all three sections. Which section shows the strongest growth trend?

3. Create a line chart of Unique Visitors by Month. How do the traffic patterns differ across the three sections?

4. Make a bar chart comparing the average Bounce Rate for all three sections. What

does this reveal about user engagement?

5. Create a line chart of Support Tickets for the Help Center. What does the trend suggest about user satisfaction over time?

6. Compare the trends across all visuals. How do engagement, traffic, and satisfaction interact for each section?

7. Identify one metric where the Blog shows improvement. Explain why this improvement matters for content strategy.

8. Identify one metric where the Store shows consistent performance. What might this stability indicate about user behavior?

9. Write one insight that connects at least two metrics for any one section (e.g., bounce rate + time on page, page views + conversions).

10. Write a two-paragraph executive summary that: • Explains the overall performance story across all three website sections • Recommends actions a manager should take based on the trends

Chapter 7

Data-Driven Business Solutions

7.1 Learning Outcomes

7-1. Connect data analysis to specific business goals using a structured approach.
7-2. Compare business options systematically and consider associated risks.
7-3. Apply basic "what-if" scenario thinking to support business decisions.
7-4. Recognize practical ways AI can enhance business decision-making.

7.2 Introduction

Sarah manages a downtown coffee shop where business has been slow lately. She knows that customers come during morning rush hour, spend more on cold drinks in summer, and that her competitor just added free Wi-Fi. But what should she actually do with this information?

This represents the real challenge in business analytics. Companies collect vast amounts of data but struggle to transform it into smart decisions. This chapter demonstrates how successful companies bridge that gap between having information and taking effective action.

7.3 Connecting Data to Business Goals

7.3.1 The Golden Rule

Data analysis only matters when it directly supports what the company is trying to accomplish. Without this connection, even the most sophisticated analysis becomes worthless effort.

Consider a pizza delivery business. If the company's goal is expanding into new neighborhoods, data analysis should focus on identifying areas with the greatest customer potential, examining population density, ordering patterns, and proximity to existing locations. However, if the goal is encouraging current customers to order more frequently, the same data would be used differently analyzing which customers might stop ordering, understanding what drives customer loyalty, and determining what changes could increase satisfaction.

7.3.2 Three-Step Process

Connecting data analysis to business goals works most effectively when you follow a clear, structured approach:

Step 1: Understand the situation by examining what is happening both inside and outside the company, including market conditions, customer needs, competitor actions, and internal capabilities.

Step 2: Decide what to analyze by identifying the specific questions that need answers and limiting your analysis to information that directly supports the decision being made.

Step 3: Plan how the results will be used by considering who will make the decision, how they will interpret the findings, and what actions they are likely to take.

7.3.3 Working Across Departments

Data-driven solutions rarely belong to just one department. Marketing focuses on attracting customers, operations concentrates on efficiency, finance aims to maximize profits, and technology maintains reliable systems. These differing priorities can make it challenging to turn analytical insights into coordinated action.

For example, if data analysis reveals that customers want faster delivery, every department plays a crucial role. Marketing must communicate the faster service, operations need to adjust workflows, technology must update tracking systems, and finance must evaluate profitability. Success requires translating insights into language each department understands and helping everyone see how their contributions support the overall business goal.

7.4 Comparing Business Options

When businesses face important decisions, they often have several possible paths forward. Rather than relying on gut feelings, effective organizations use structured approaches to compare their options fairly.

7.4.1 Smart Decision Process

A smart decision process begins by identifying all possible choices, including creative alternatives. Decision-makers then determine which factors matter most, such as financial impact, strategic alignment, and practical feasibility. Each option is evaluated consistently using these factors, and assumptions are tested by considering what might happen if key expectations prove wrong.

A restaurant chain deciding how to grow provides a clear example:

Option	Investment	Revenue Potential	Risk	Timeline
New Locations	500,000	300,000	High	12 months
Delivery Service	50,000	150,000	Medium	3 months

Option	Investment	Revenue Potential	Risk	Timeline
Menu Expansion	25,000	75,000	Low	1 month

7.4.2 Weighted Scoring for Complex Decisions

When multiple factors influence a decision, weighted scoring provides a structured comparison method. This approach identifies factors that matter most and assigns each one a weight based on its importance. Each option is then scored on each factor using the same scale.

For example, in software selection, cost might represent 30% of the decision, ease of use 25%, and features 20%. By multiplying each score by its assigned weight and adding the results, decision-makers can calculate an overall score for each option. This method makes trade-offs explicit and ensures that the final choice reflects what truly matters most to the organization.

7.4.3 Managing Risk

Every business decision involves risk—the possibility that outcomes will differ from expectations. Organizations can avoid risk by selecting safer options, reduce risk through careful planning and testing, transfer risk through insurance or partnerships, or accept risk while preparing backup plans.

The key insight is that avoiding all risk is rarely desirable, since it often means missing valuable opportunities. Instead, businesses should understand the risks they are taking, ensure that potential rewards justify those risks, and be prepared to respond effectively if conditions change.

7.5 Building "What-If" Models

Business decisions are often made under uncertainty. "What-if" models are analytical tools that help decision-makers explore possible outcomes before committing real resources, allowing businesses to test ideas and evaluate strategies in a controlled environment.

7.5.1 Simple Scenario Models

What-if models are simplified representations of how a business operates, focusing on the most important factors that drive outcomes. Think of them as a video game version of a business, where strategies can be tested repeatedly without real-world consequences.

Consider a coffee shop that wants to understand what drives monthly revenue. A simple model might calculate: Monthly Revenue = Customers per Day × Average Spend × Days Open. This basic equation allows the owner to explore scenarios like increasing prices by 10%, extending operating hours, or adding a loyalty program.

7.5.2 Types of Business Scenarios

To make what-if analysis more systematic, businesses often organize scenarios into common categories:

Scenario	Purpose	Example
Best Case	Plan for success	High adoption, low costs
Worst Case	Prepare backup plans	Cultural barriers, high costs
Most Likely	Form main plan	Moderate adoption, expected costs
Stress Test	Test resilience	Economic recession

For example, an online store considering international expansion might define its best-case scenario as high customer adoption with favorable exchange rates, while the worst-case scenario could involve cultural misunderstandings and regulatory challenges. Together, these scenarios provide a comprehensive view of possible outcomes.

7.5.3 Making Models Practical

For what-if models to be useful, they must balance simplicity with relevance. Models should focus on key factors that have the greatest impact on outcomes rather than attempting to include every possible variable. Interactive models allow users to easily change inputs and immediately see how outcomes respond.

The primary goal of what-if modeling is not to predict the future with perfect accuracy, but to improve understanding of how different factors affect outcomes so that better decisions can be made.

7.6 Using AI for Business Optimization

7.6.1 What AI Can Do for Business Decisions

Artificial Intelligence functions like an exceptionally capable assistant that can process enormous amounts of data, identify patterns humans might miss, and test thousands of scenarios quickly. AI excels at finding patterns, massive scenario testing, real-time optimization, and prediction using historical data.

7.6.2 Simple AI Applications

You don't need technical expertise to use AI for business decisions. Common applications include:

AI Application	Purpose / How It Helps
Inventory Management	Predicts needed stock based on sales patterns and external factors
Pricing Optimization	Analyzes competitor prices and customer behavior for optimal pricing
Customer Segmentation	Groups customers by behavior patterns rather than simple demographics
Employee Scheduling	Balances labor costs, employee preferences, skills, and service needs
Marketing Optimization	Determines which customers to target with which messages

7.6.3 Getting Started and Understanding Limitations

Start small with one specific problem where you have good data. Use existing AI tools in business software before building custom solutions. Focus on data quality, since AI is only as good as the data you provide.

AI limitations include complete dependence on data quality, inability to explain recommendations in many systems, reliance on historical patterns that may not apply if conditions change, and the continued need for human judgment in final decisions. Use AI to enhance human decision-making, not replace it.

7.7 Practical Application: Restaurant Chain Expansion

A regional restaurant chain with 15 locations wants 50% revenue growth in two years. Their options include new locations, new markets, delivery services, franchising, or new concepts. They evaluate using revenue potential, investment requirements, risk levels, timing, and strategic fit.

They build simple models for each option, test different scenarios (best case, worst case, most likely), and use AI tools for customer analysis and location optimization. Their final recommendation considers quantitative results, qualitative factors like brand fit, and risk tolerance given available resources.

7.8 Conclusion

Collecting data is only the first step; the real challenge—and opportunity—lies in transforming that data into decisions that drive meaningful business outcomes. Successful organizations bridge this gap by systematically connecting analysis to clearly defined business goals, ensuring that every insight has a practical purpose. Structured decision-making tools, like weighted scoring, allow businesses to compare options fairly, consider trade-offs, and make choices that reflect both strategic priorities and operational realities. At the same time, scenario planning and what-if modeling help decision-makers anticipate uncertainty, test strategies safely, and prepare for a range of possible outcomes, turning risk into manageable insight rather than guesswork.

Artificial intelligence further enhances this process by processing large datasets, identifying patterns that humans might overlook, and simulating multiple scenarios quickly, yet it is most effective when paired with human judgment rather than used in isolation. Cross-functional collaboration is equally essential, as translating analytical insights into action often requires marketing, operations, finance, and technology teams to work together, aligning their efforts toward a shared goal. By combining strategic alignment, systematic evaluation, scenario planning, and AI-assisted insights, businesses can move beyond intuition, make more informed decisions, and respond more effectively to changing conditions. Ultimately, the ability to turn data into actionable business decisions is not just a competitive advantage—it is a fundamental skill for anyone looking to create real impact in a data-driven world.

7.9 Key Terms

Data-Driven Decision Making: Using data systematically to guide business actions rather than relying on intuition.

Three-Step Process: A structured approach to connect data analysis to business goals: Understand the situation, Decide what to analyze, Plan how results will be used.

Weighted Scoring: A method to compare multiple options by scoring each factor and applying relative importance weights.

Risk Management: Identifying, evaluating, and planning for uncertainties that could impact business decisions.

What-If Model: An analytical tool that simulates different scenarios to explore potential business outcomes.

Scenario Planning: Developing best-case, worst-case, most likely, and stress-test scenarios to prepare for uncertainties.

Artificial Intelligence (AI): Technology that processes large data sets, identifies patterns, tests scenarios, and supports decision-making.

Inventory Management (AI Application): Predicts needed stock based on sales patterns and external factors.

Pricing Optimization (AI Application): Analyzes competitor prices and customer behavior to suggest optimal pricing.

Customer Segmentation (AI Application): Groups customers by behavior patterns rather than simple demographics.

Employee Scheduling (AI Application): Balances labor costs, employee preferences, skills, and service needs.

Marketing Optimization (AI Application): Determines which customers to target with which messages for maximum impact.

7.10 Review Questions

1. **Application:** A retail company wants to reduce customer complaints. Using the three-step process, what would you do in each step to connect data analysis to this business goal?

2. **Analysis:** You're choosing between three marketing strategies with different costs, reach, and conversion rates. How would you use weighted scoring to make this decision?
3. **Scenario Planning:** A startup is launching a new app. What four types of scenarios should they model, and what might each scenario include?
4. **AI Implementation:** A small restaurant wants to use AI for the first time. What would be a good starting application and why?
5. **Risk Management:** A company is considering expanding internationally. What are three types of risks they should consider and one strategy for managing each?
6. **Integration:** How would you explain to a marketing manager why they need to work with operations and finance teams to implement a data-driven solution for faster customer service?

7.11 Lab 7-1 Data-Driven Business Solutions

In this lab, you will learn how to connect data to business goals, compare strategic options, and use what-if modeling to make data-driven recommendations.

7.11.1 Demonstration

Sarah manages a downtown coffee shop. She wants to explore strategies to improve revenue. You will analyze possible options, evaluate risk and return, and test what-if scenarios.

Table 7.4: Strategic investment options with financial and risk profile

Option	Investment	Revenue Potential	Risk	Timeline (Months)
New Locations	500000	300000	High	12
Delivery Service	50000	150000	Medium	3
Menu Expansion	25000	75000	Low	1

7.11.1.1 Step 1: Calculate Net Potential Revenue

Net revenue potential is the amount of money a business expects to gain after subtracting the cost of an investment from the revenue it could generate. It helps determine whether an idea is financially worthwhile by showing if the expected earnings exceed the initial cost.

To calculate net revenue potential, you subtract the investment from the revenue potential using the formula: Net Revenue Potential = Revenue Potential − Investment. A positive result indicates a profit, while a negative result indicates a loss.

In Excel, you first enter the data into columns such as Investment and Revenue Potential. Then, in a new column labeled Net Revenue Potential, you type a formula like =C2 − B2 to subtract the investment from the revenue. After pressing Enter, you can drag the formula down to calculate the result for the other options.

Table 7.5: Financial comparison of strategic options

Option	Investment	Revenue Potential	Net Revenue Potential
New Locations	500000	300000	-200000
Delivery Service	50000	150000	100000
Menu Expansion	25000	75000	50000

7.11.1.2 Step 2: Discuss risk vs reward for each option

Each option shows a different balance between risk and reward, so the best choice depends on how much uncertainty Sarah is willing to accept.

New Locations has a high risk and negative reward in the short term. It requires a large investment of $500,000 but only generates $300,000 in potential revenue, resulting in a loss of $200,000. While it might lead to long-term growth, the immediate financial return is poor and the risk is high due to the large upfront cost and longer timeline.

Delivery Service offers a moderate risk with the highest reward. With an investment of $50,000 and a net gain of $100,000, it provides strong returns in a relatively short time (3 months). The medium risk reflects some uncertainty, but the payoff makes it an attractive and balanced option.

Menu Expansion has low risk and a smaller but positive reward. It only requires $25,000 and generates a $50,000 net gain. Although the profit is lower than delivery service, it is safer and faster to implement (1 month), making it a stable and low-risk improvement.

Overall, delivery service provides the best balance of risk and return, while menu expansion is the safest option, and new locations is the riskiest with no immediate financial benefit.

7.11.1.3 Step 3: Evaluate using weighted scoring

Weighted scoring compares all options using a single score by combining investment, revenue potential, risk, and timeline with different importance levels. The weights used are 30% for investment, 40% for revenue potential, 20% for risk, and 10% for timeline. However, before Excel can calculate anything, all values must be in numeric form, because Excel cannot process words like “High,” “Medium,” or “Low.”

To fix this, risk and timeline must be converted into numbers. A common scoring system is to make higher numbers better. For risk, “High” becomes 1, “Medium” becomes

3, and "Low" becomes 5 because lower risk is better. For timeline, longer time gets a lower score, so 12 months becomes 1, 3 months becomes 4, and 1 month becomes 5. This allows all factors to be measured on the same scale. Investment and revenue are also converted into scores on the same 1–5 scale, where lower investment receives a higher score and higher revenue receives a higher score.

Table 7.6: Strategic option scoring matrix

Option	Investment Score	Revenue Score	Risk Score	Timeline Score
New Locations	1	3	1	1
Delivery Service	4	4	3	4
Menu Expansion	5	2	5	5

Once everything is converted into scores, Excel calculates the weighted score by multiplying each score by its weight and adding them together. For example, for New Locations, the formula becomes:

=(InvestmentScore × 0.3) + (RevenueScore × 0.4) + (RiskScore × 0.2) + (TimelineScore × 0.1)

So, if New Locations has scores of 1 for investment, 3 for revenue, 1 for risk, and 1 for timeline, the calculation would be:

=(1×0.3) + (3×0.4) + (1×0.2) + (1×0.1) = 1.8

This gives a final weighted score of 1.8, which reflects all factors together in one value. The same process is repeated for Delivery Service and Menu Expansion so they can be compared fairly, and the highest score shows the best overall option based on all weighted criteria.

Table 7.7: Weighted decision matrix for strategic options

Option	Investment Score	Revenue Score	Risk Score	Timeline Score	Overall Score
New Locations	1	3	1	1	1.8
Delivery Service	4	4	3	4	3.8
Menu Expansion	5	2	5	5	3.8

The results show that Delivery Service and Menu Expansion are tied at 3.8, meaning they are equally strong overall when using the assigned weights. This happens because both options balance the criteria differently: Delivery Service performs strongly in revenue and has moderate scores elsewhere, while Menu Expansion performs very well in investment, risk, and timeline but has lower revenue potential.

In cases like this, a tie does not mean the analysis is incorrect; it simply means the decision depends on which factor is considered more important in practice. For example, if revenue growth is prioritized more heavily, Delivery Service may be preferred. If lower cost, lower risk, and faster implementation are more important, Menu Expansion may be the better choice.

Overall, weighted scoring helps highlight that multiple options can be similarly strong, and final decision-making may require adjusting priorities or reviewing weights.

7.11.1.4 Step 4: Perform a what-if scenario

A what-if scenario in Excel is used to test how sensitive financial results are to small changes in assumptions. Instead of relying on a single fixed calculation, it allows different possible outcomes to be explored to reflect real-world uncertainty. In this task, the purpose is to analyse how Net Potential Revenue changes when both revenue and investment do not remain constant and may vary slightly.

To complete this in Excel, you begin with the existing dataset where Net Potential Revenue has already been calculated using the formula Revenue minus Investment. Once this base calculation is in place, two additional columns are added next to it: one for a best-case scenario and one for a worst-case scenario. These columns show how results change when assumptions are adjusted.

For the best-case scenario, a realistic improvement in business performance is assumed. Revenue is increased by 10% to reflect higher sales due to stronger demand or improved conditions. Investment is increased by 5% to reflect possible small cost increases. In Excel, this is calculated by multiplying revenue by 1.10 and investment by 1.05, then subtracting the adjusted investment from the adjusted revenue.

For the worst-case scenario, a less favourable outcome is considered. Revenue is reduced by 10% to reflect lower sales, while investment is reduced by 5% to reflect slightly lower spending. In Excel, this is calculated by multiplying revenue by 0.90 and investment by 0.95, then subtracting the adjusted investment from the adjusted revenue.

After applying these calculations, the results are:

Table 7.8: Scenario analysis of strategic options (net revenue outcomes)

Option	Original Net Revenue Potential	Best Case	Worst Case
New Locations	-200000	-155000	-245000

Option	Original Net Revenue Potential	Best Case	Worst Case
Delivery Service	100000	112500	85000
Menu Expansion	50000	57500	42500

The results show clear differences in performance under changing conditions. New Locations remains negative in all scenarios, meaning it consistently results in a loss and becomes even less viable in the worst-case scenario. Delivery Service performs the strongest overall, showing the highest profit in both normal and best-case scenarios and still maintaining a positive result even in the worst case. Menu Expansion is the most stable option, with relatively small changes between best and worst cases, indicating low risk but also lower profit potential compared to Delivery Service.

Overall, the what-if analysis shows that Delivery Service is the best balance of profitability and resilience, Menu Expansion is the safest but lower-return option, and New Locations is the highest risk and least financially viable option under changing conditions.

7.11.2 Practice

Your small gym is considering several ways to grow membership and revenue. Using the data below, perform the same analysis steps as the demo.

Table 7.9: Business investment options with projected returns and risk

Option	Invest.	RevenuePotential	Risk	Time(Mos.)
Add New Equipment	20000	45000	Low	1
Open Evening Classes	10000	30000	Medium	2
Launch Personal Training	15000	50000	Medium	1
Introduce Yoga Studio	25000	60000	High	3
Nutrition Coaching	12000	25000	Low	1
Summer Bootcamp	8000	20000	Low	1

7.11.2.1 Questions

1. Calculate Net Potential Revenue = Revenue Potential - Investment for each option.
2. Create a bar chart comparing Net Potential for all options.
3. Discuss risk vs reward: which options have high revenue potential but also high risk?
4. Perform weighted scoring using the following weights: Investment 25%, Revenue Potential 40%, Risk 25%, and Timeline 10%, and calculate the final weighted score for each option in Excel.

5. Conduct a what-if scenario in Excel by recalculating results assuming revenue varies by ±15% and investment varies by ±10%, and show the impact on outcomes.

6. Prepare a short Word report that includes an executive summary (3–4 sentences highlighting key findings), context explaining why the analysis matters for the gym, key insights identifying the most promising options and why, and clear recommendations on which actions the gym should take. Include relevant Excel tables and charts to support your conclusions.

www.ingramcontent.com/pod-product-compliance
Lightning Source LLC
Chambersburg PA
CBHW061355240926
51846CB00007B/1413
* 9 7 8 1 9 6 9 2 3 3 4 0 1 *